Penn Greek Drama Series

Series Editors
David R. Slavitt
Palmer Bovie

The Penn Greek Drama Series presents fresh literary translations of the entire corpus of classical Greek drama: tragedies, comedies, and satyr plays. The only contemporary series of all the surviving work of Aeschylus, Sophocles, Euripides, Aristophanes, and Menander, this collection brings together men and women of literary distinction whose versions of the plays in contemporary English poetry can be acted on the stage or in the individual reader's theater of the mind.

The aim of the series is to make this cultural treasure accessible, restoring as faithfully as possible the original luster of the plays and offering in living verse a view of what talented contemporary poets have seen in their readings of these works so fundamental a part of Western civilization.

Euripides, 1

Medea, Hecuba, Andromache,
The Bacchae

Edited by
David R. Slavitt and Palmer Bovie

PENN
University of Pennsylvania Press
Philadelphia

Copyright © 1998 University of Pennsylvania Press
The Bacchae copyright © 1998 Daniel Mark Epstein
All rights reserved
Printed in the United States of America on acid-free paper

10 9 8 7 6 5 4 3 2 1

Published by
University of Pennsylvania Press
Philadelphia, Pennsylvania 19104-4011

Library of Congress Cataloging-in-Publication Data

Euripides.
    [Works. English. 1997]
    Euripides / edited by David R. Slavitt and Palmer Bovie.
        p.   cm.—(Penn Greek drama series)
    Contents: 1. Medea. Hecuba. Andromache. The Bacchae—2. Hippolytus.
Suppliant women. Helen. Electra. Cyclops
        ISBN 0-8122-3415-4 (v. 1 : cloth : alk. paper).—ISBN 0-8122-1626-1
(v. 1 : pbk. : alk. paper).—ISBN 0-8122-3421-9 (v. 2 : cloth : alk. paper).—
ISBN 0-8122-1629-6 (v. 2 : pbk. : alk. paper)
        1. Euripides—Translations into English.   2. Greek drama (Tragedy)—
Translations into English.   3. Mythology, Greek—Drama.   I. Series.
PA3975.A1   1997
882'.01—dc21   97-28892
                                                                              CIP

Contents

Introduction

Palmer Bovie

Classical Greek tragedy, which flourished in Athens during the fifth century B.C., grew out of country festivals originating a century earlier. Three different celebrations in honor of Dionysus, known as the rural Dionysia, occurred during the winter months. One of these, the Lenaea, was also observed at Athens in the sanctuary of Dionysus. In addition to song it offered ecstatic dances and comedy. Another, the Anthesteria, lasted for three days as a carnival time of revelry and wine drinking. It also included a remembrance of the dead and was believed to be connected with Orestes' mythical return to Athens purged of guilt for killing his mother Clytemnestra.

The rural Dionysia were communal holidays observed to honor Dionysus, the god of wine, of growth and fertility, and of lightning. Free-spirited processions to an altar of Dionysus were crowned by lyrical odes to the god sung by large choruses of men and boys chanting responsively under the direction of their leader. The ritual included the sacrifice of a goat at the god's altar, from which the term "tragedy," meaning goat-song, may derive. Gradually themes of a more serious nature gained ground over the joyful, exuberant addresses to the liberating god, legends of familiar heroes, and mythological tales of divine retribution. But the undercurrent of the driving Dionysiac spirit was seldom absent, even in the sophisticated artistry of the masterful tragic poets of the fifth century.

Initially the musical texts were antiphonal exchanges between the chorus and its leader. Thespis, who won the prize of a goat for tragedy at Athens in 534 B.C., is traditionally said to have been the first to appear as an actor, separate from the chorus, speaking a prologue and making set speeches, with his face variously disguised by a linen mask. A fourth festival, the City Dionysia or the Great Dionysia, was instituted by the ruler Peisistratus, also in 534, and nine years later Aeschylus was born. It seems that the major era of Greek tragic art was destined to begin.

The Great Dionysia, an annual occasion for dramatic competitions in tragedy and comedy, was held in honor of Dionysus Eleutheros. Its five-day celebration began with a procession in which the statue of Dionysus was carried to the nearby village of Eleutherai (the site of the Eleusinian Mysteries) and then back, in a parade by torchlight, to Athens and the precincts of Dionysus on the lower slopes of the Acropolis. In the processional ranks were city officials, young men of military age leading a bull, foreign residents of Athens wearing scarlet robes, and participants in the dramatic contests, including the producers (*choregoi*), resplendent in colorful costumes. The ceremonies ended with the sacrificial slaughter of the bull and the installation of Dionysus' statue on his altar at the center of the orchestra.

For three days each of the poets chosen for the competition presented his work, three tragedies and one satyr play (a farcical comedy performed in the afternoon after an interval following the staging of tragedies). In the late afternoon comedies were offered. The other two days were marked by dithyrambic competitions, five boys' choruses on one day, five men's on the other. The dithyramb, earlier an excited dramatic dance, became in the Athenian phase a quieter performance, sung by a chorus of fifty and offering little movement.

The theater of Dionysus at Athens was an outdoor space on the southern slope of the Acropolis. A semicircular auditorium was created on the hillside from stone or marble slabs, or shaped from the natural rock with wooden seats added. Narrow stepways gave access to the seats, the front row of which could be fitted out with marble chairs for official or distinguished members of the audience. From sites visible today at Athens, Delphi, Epidaurus, and elsewhere, it is evident that the sloping amphitheater had excellent acoustic properties and that the voices of the actors and the chorus were readily heard.

The acting area began with an *orchestra*, a circular space some sixty feet in diameter where the chorus performed its dance movements, voiced its commentaries, and engaged in dialogue with the actors. In the center of the orchestra was an altar of Dionysus, and on it a statue of the god. Behind the orchestra several steps led to a stage platform in front of the *skene*, a wooden building with a central door and doors at each end and a flat roof. The actors could enter and exit through these doors or one of the sides, retiring to assume different masks and costumes for a change of role. They could also appear on the roof for special effects, as in Euripides' *Orestes* where at the end Orestes and Pylades appear, menacing Helen with death, before she is whisked away from them by Apollo. The skene's facade represented a palace or temple and could have an altar in front of it. Stage properties included the *eccyclema*, a wheeled platform that was rolled out from the central door or the side of the skene to display an interior setting or a tableau, as at the end of Aeschylus' *Agamemnon* where the murdered bodies of Agamemnon and Cassandra are proudly displayed by Clytemnestra.

Another piece of equipment occasionally brought into play was the *mechane*, a tall crane that could lift an actor or heavy objects (e.g., Medea in her chariot) high above the principals' heads. This device, also known as the *deus ex machina*, was favored by Euripides who, in the climactic scene of *Orestes* shows Apollo protecting Helen in the air high above Orestes and Pylades on the roof. Or a deity may appear above the stage to resolve a final conflict and bring the plot to a successful conclusion, as the figure of Athena does at the end of Euripides' *Iphigenia in Tauris*. Sections of background at each end of the stage could be revolved to indicate a change of scene. These *periaktoi*, triangular in shape, could be shown to the audience to indicate a change of place or, together with thunder and lightning machines, could announce the appearance of a god.

The actors wore masks that characterized their roles and could be changed offstage to allow one person to play several different parts in the same drama. In the earliest period tragedy was performed by only one actor in counterpoint with the chorus, as could be managed, for example, in Aeschylus' *Suppliants*. But Aeschylus himself introduced the role of a second actor, simultaneously present on the stage, Sophocles made use of a third, and he and Euripides probably a fourth. From such simple elements (the orchestra space for the chorus, the slightly raised stage and its scene front, the minimal cast of actors) was created the astonishingly powerful poetic drama of the fifth-century Athenian poets.

What we can read and see today is but a small fraction of the work produced by the three major poets and a host of fellow artists who presented plays in the dramatic competitions. Texts of tragedies of Aeschylus, Sophocles, and Euripides were copied and stored in public archives at Athens, along with Aristophanes' comedies. At some later point a selection was made of the surviving plays, seven by Aeschylus, seven by Sophocles, nine by Euripides, and ten others of his discovered by chance. In the late third and early second centuries B.C., this collection of thirty-three plays was conveyed to the great library of Alexandria, where scholarly commentaries, *scholia*, formed part of the canon, to be copied and transmitted to students and readers in the Greco-Roman cultural world.

Euripides (485–406 B.C.) was born near Athens, the son of prosperous middle-class parents. He spent most of his life in study and in writing his poetry "in a cave by the sea in Salamis." At Athens his associates included Archelaus, a pupil of the philosopher Anaxagoras, Protagoras, Prodicus, and Socrates. Such acquaintances, cited by early biographers, are well worth considering in view of Euripides' flair for weaving philosophical debates into many dramatic dialogues, or marshaling logical principles in set speeches. During the oppressive decades of the Peloponnesian War, Euripides may have incurred the hostility of his fellow citizens by his denunciation of war and its havoc, a recurrent theme in many of his plays. For whatever reason, he withdrew into retirement, living a rather unsociable existence. For his conventional treatment of mythological figures and situations he was mercilessly mocked by the comic poets, especially Aristophanes. And his skeptical approach to standard religious conceptions may have disturbed many of his listeners. Late in life, three or four years before his death, Euripides left Athens for residence, first, in Magnesia and then in Macedon at the court of King Archelaus, where he was received with great honor. There he continued writing plays, his last work being *The Bacchae*, a dramatic limning of the dire consequences of abandoning belief in Dionysus.

Euripides differs from his fellow playwrights in several ways. He adopts unusual versions from the repertory of myth, and his plots and characters are often so realistically developed as to seem new and modern rather than classical. Often we see his principals escape from their predicaments. Fate turns out to be the unexpected. The chorus may interact with the players or its lyrics may form a descant on themes quite separate from the action in progress. In the fluent and quick-witted play of ideas, skepticism can override belief and logic and challenge simple convictions.

His *Electra* varies from the versions of Aeschylus and Sophocles in its astonishing recharacterization of Electra as now married to a peasant farmer who treats her with respect and honors her chastity. Their simple country hut becomes the scene of Clytemnestra's murder. Electra summons her mother on the pretext of having borne a child and wanting her there to perform the ritual of cleansing. With this ironic, macabre embellishment on the conventional murder scene, Euripides seems to be actually increasing the guilt felt by the children. But until this point Electra's conduct as the humble helpmeet of a husband with a heart of gold outclasses her mourning. She smolders with resentment but bides her time, waiting for Orestes, hoping. That Euripides sees her in a different light is also signaled in his refuting the others' recognition tokens. A lock of hair, a scrap of child's clothing, footprints? Absurd to think of such things as clues to Orestes' identity! What he can be known by is the scar on his forehead, "where he was cut in a fall, chasing a fawn with you in his father's courtyard." So tangible and realistic a memory convinces Electra. The fact is that Orestes is scarred for life. His identification was not just a clever bit of literary criticism.

Brother and sister are, at the end of the *Electra*, brought to the depth of sorrow by the realization of what they have done. But they are lifted out of despair by the timely appearance of their divine relatives Castor and Polydeuces, *ex machina*. The Dioscuri, the heavenly Twins, have paused in their rush "to seas off Sicily, to protect the ships in danger there." Athens had sent an expedition to the aid of the fleet in Sicily in 413, so it appears that Euripides is being historical as well as mythical here. Electra is to leave Argos and marry Pylades, to live in exile. Orestes must go to Athens and await trial at the Areopagus. The children's generation, marked by the ancient curse of violence on their house, has nevertheless emerged to survive. The Dioscuri (Castor and Polydeuces were the divine brothers of Helen and Clytemnestra) also report, almost casually, that Menelaus and Helen will attend to the burial rites for Clytemnestra and Aegisthus. They explain that Menelaus and Helen have recently arrived from Egypt. She, Helen, never went to Troy, they add laconically.

The year 412 saw the production of Euripides' drama *Helen*, which offers the counter-myth that Hermes had spirited Helen away to Egypt, substituting for her at Troy a phantom image. In Egypt she enjoyed the protection of the king, Proteus, during the ten years of the Trojan war, but after his death his son holds her hostage and wants to make her his wife. She fends him off by maintaining a constant vigil at Proteus' tomb, a sacred refuge. This story line, sketched in by Helen in the prologue in her play, was suggested earlier by an episode in Book II, the Egyptian book, of Herodotus' *Histories*, and poems in praise of Helen by Stesichorus and other sixth-century lyric poets in Euripides' combination. He has seized the opportunity to dramatize Helen's rescue, starting with her joyful reunion with Menelaus, who has been shipwrecked with his crew and the phantom Helen on these shores. Her meeting with him surely constitutes the most appealing recognition scene of any in the Greek drama we know, and Euripides weaves a spell of exciting suspense as husband and wife devise the strategy for eluding their Egyptian captor. Plans are made and discarded until finally Helen hits on the right tactics, saying (almost under her breath) "Wait, I have a good suggestion." Their daring plan enables husband and wife to escape from impending doom, and Helen from captivity and slander.

Another Euripidean heroine to escape from peril is found in *Iphigenia in Tauris*. Orestes and Pylades join forces with Iphigenia in devising a plan to outwit the barbarous king of Thrace and sail away to Athens. The men supply the force, the woman the strategic plan. Men may be forceful, Euripides implies, but women are more resourceful. In other female figures, like Ion's mother in the *Ion* and Alcestis in the *Alcestis*, women are rescued from tragedy. Alcestis, indeed, is wrested from the arms of Death by Heracles and restored to her husband's embrace.

Euripides explores the complex dimensions of female character from many angles. In plays from the Trojan War cycle, women are towering figures of tragic sorrow as they voice the grief that descends on the victims of war. Swept up in the grotesque futility of war, the Trojan women endure further humiliation in the senseless murders of their children in the war's catastrophic aftermath. Small wonder that we should weep for Hecuba. A later representation of Andromache finds her married to Neoptolemus, Achilles' son, and having borne a son to him. As if this irony were not insult added to injury, Andromache is now threatened with murder by the new mistress who has replaced her. She is protected by Peleus (a Trojan Woman saved by a Trojan Man), but Menelaus and Hermione, the new mistress, are still bent on doing her in. At the melodramatic moment, Orestes arrives on the scene and will despatch Neoptolemus, taking Hermione as his bride. Here Euripides has ingeniously rescued two women from imminent destruction, one Trojan and one Greek, Hermione being the daughter of

Helen. He evidently found such figures as the poignant Andromache and the jealousy-ridden rival Hermione well worth close attention.

The poet's fascinating portraits of celebrated women drawn from the mythological traditions rises to the level of Aeschylean or Sophoclean theatricality. While he may not invoke the grandeur of Aeschylus' vision or the nobility of Sophocles' unerring judgment, Euripides offers his audience real life human beings, natural characters under, at times, supernatural pressures. His memorable women Medea and Phaedra become avenging forces and are demonically driven to destroy the source of their happiness. They do not gain wisdom through suffering, but plunge into darkness. Medea may fly off to Athens in a chariot drawn by dragons, but in reality her burden is her murdered children and all she and Jason once cherished. Her husband is ruined: she, almost worse, is deluded. What she said of herself turns out to be true—"rage will bite through reason's curb." Phaedra's psychological burden in the *Hippolytus* is shame and guilt. Her lust humiliates her and compels her to bring disgrace on the innocent young hero. His devotion to Artemis conflicts with her subjection to Aphrodite: both Hippolytus and Phaedra are destroyed in the clash of wills. Tragedy is, of course, the truth realized too late: and too late Theseus discovers his son's innocence and his wife's aberration.

From a terrifying view of women driven to a demonic state we find, in *The Bacchae*, Euripides' last play, what can be considered a misogynist stance. But on the whole this brutal drama chiefly brings to mind the peril of denying an underlying neutral power, the life force that of necessity controls all beings. That is, Dionysus, whose cosmic energy animates life and whose passionate powers motivate the "drama," the forward motion registered by Greek tragedy.

Toward men as heroes Euripides' attitude is sometimes disparaging. The men in *Iphigenia in Aulis* are hardly impressive as they assemble to sail against Troy. Only Achilles achieves some stature, and all are far below the unblemished radiance of Iphigenia, their victim. And Orestes, in the tragedy named after him, is frantic, haunted by his guilty conscience; he plunges wildly into futile gestures of revenge. Heracles can be driven mad and returns to his senses, chastened but none the wiser. In the first play of which we have a record, the *Alcestis*, produced at Athens in 438 B.C. and winner of second prize in the contest at the Great Dionysia, Euripides plays woman against man, wife against husband. The drama itself was in fact the fourth of the group offered, in place of a satyr play. But it does not function as a satyr play; rather, it sets the stage for a reconciliation of an ordinary man and his extraordinary wife. Alcestis has offered to die in her husband's stead, and it is only when Death leads her off the stage that her husband Admetus realizes what he has lost by his wrongminded acceptance of Alcestis' sacrificial gesture. Luckily, Heracles has come to visit his friend Admetus, who, in his characteristically hospitable manner, receives him cordially and hides his knowledge of Alcestis' death. But Heracles learns the truth and it is not too late: he strides off to confront Death, wrests Alcestis from the fatal grasp, and leads back a veiled female figure. He places her in Admetus' hands, instructing his host not to raise the veil until three days have passed. The bulky hero leaves. The play ends. We realize that this well-intentioned but blundering man and his somber, self-denying wife were well worth being saved from their tragic destiny, as the chorus exits, singing:

> The Powers take on many shapes;
> the gods accomplish miracles.
> What was predicted fails to happen,
> then gods reveal their hidden design:
> —and this was what took place.

Medea

Translated by
Eleanor Wilner with Inés Azar

Translator's Preface

This *Medea* is not the one I remember teaching twenty-five or more years ago. "The eye altering," says Blake, "alters all." And certainly my eyes have changed in those years. As has the world, and the world view. Then, too, there is the matter of translation. When you are finding new language for a play, even more than a director or an actor who takes it on, you must move inside the drama, into its inner workings—its characters, its plot, and what coils under the plot and, as it unwinds, provides the play's spring.

For wherever it may lead, I want to try to track here the difference between the earlier *Medea* I taught with youthful fervor and the *Medea* I discover now as its translator, late in this bloody century and in the sixth decade of my own life. The earlier Medea, the character, as I recalled her, was a figure for the betrayed woman and proto-feminist, the superior alien treated as inferior barbarian, the foreigner without rights or protection, and, in her connection with older gods and natural forces, an avatar of nature's revenge on an Athens represented by the sometime hero Jason and his sophistries—a power grown cold, opportunist, imperial, and corrupt. In short, Euripides' best-known play was modern in its skepticism and reading of motivation, psychologically acute, sympathetic to the Other (a concept still fresh with dew in the literary and philosophic discourse of the 1950s and '60s), and also an allegory for the Greek world of 431 B.C., the year of *Medea*'s production being the opening year of the long, self-destructive Peloponnesian War, which would destroy the future of Athenian hegemony even as Medea destroys her children. The play was part parable, part admonition. Sunk in the turbulence of its passionate chaos, deep enough for tragic import, was a solid ethical mooring to which we could tie our demand for meaning.

We believed—we being myself and the literary scholars who influenced me more than I realized—that the Classical works that endured must have provided such moral moorage in the waters of time. Wasn't that what constituted tradition? I realize now that back then both this reader, and the critics and scholars of Classical literature whose readings provided the prevailing lenses through which the work was seen, had one thing in common: piety. And piety, which was the built-in attitude toward all the Classical authors and other monuments on which Western culture founded its sense of original genius and continuous identity, was precisely—I now think—the most misleading lens through which to view a drama whose central target is piety, along with heroism, belief in moral order, and high or happy expectations of any kind whatsoever. Translating the play was to open a kind of Pandora's box without the butterfly of hope, and to raise anew the question of what it is that lasts.

The Chorus, Jason, Creon, and Medea all mouth pieties their actions or their next speech belie. The difference between Medea and the other characters in this regard is that she is aware of her (and their) duplicity, and uses that awareness to manipulate the others. She knows well the weaknesses their vaunted or pious words conceal—and plays on the particular vanities of each character. She is a Machiavel without a country to rule—her cause is her own injured pride and power, and the tragedy of Medea, if tragedy is indeed the right word for this brand of truth, is not only that her scale is outsize for the scope of her role in life, but that the logic of the perfect revenge of the cornered person has a Samson-like side—her revenge is surgically exquisite, her enemies are destroyed, and, in a manner of speaking, she has pulled down the house on her own head.

Her house had, of course, been her cage, even as her sense of humiliation was sharpened by her circumstantial dependence on a hollow man into whom her passionate nature and thwarted power once poured full force, a husband for whom she has obvious and, we can surmise, longstanding contempt. From such a power imbalance—she having the innate, he the institutionalized power—comes the time-honored saying "Hell hath no fury like a woman scorned." To understand that, it is necessary to hear simultaneously under that last phrase another—"like a woman's scorn." It surfaces in Medea's clear statement of the purpose of all this blood: "But what is grief compared to the ridicule of fools?"

The nihilist chill of those words reaches the bone when we recall the spilled blood from which that grief arises. The dead children are both fact and metaphor, for on what future, what innocence or principle or hero can the audience now rely? At the end of the *Medea* the future seems empty, almost unimaginable—and it is perhaps that, as much as its psychological acuity, which makes the play seem so unfortunately appropriate to our own moment. There is, as well, the equally appropriate fact that her connections with the past have twice been savagely cut by Medea's own hand, and this for the sake of her passion. In this she may be the Western original for that person who has become all too familiar to us today—the radically disconnected self pursuing personal desires in an egocentric universe.

The servants in the play—nurse, tutor, messenger—are the reliable characters, which only sharpens the bitter ironies, for they function in the play as the predictors and reliable narrators of events to which they are powerless witnesses, crimes at which they express horror but are entirely helpless to prevent. The Chorus? To the traditional caution of Greek citizen Choruses, they add a mean-spirited self-interest and barely hidden animus which are, in their way, almost as repellent as the opportunistic cowardice of Jason or the calculated crimes of the outraged and raging Medea. The very first words from the Chorus warn us of the way people take pleasure in the pain of others, and may alert us to one of the assumptions on which Euripides rests his dramaturgy, and which may be one explanation for the play's enduring popularity. Hearing the wailing cries emerge from Medea's house, they allow as how they can't take pleasure in the fall of this house, as they "have shared the cup of friendship there." There is loyalty there, yes, but also this first, and seemingly unwitting revelation of sadistic excitement as a commonplace.

The Chorus reveal themselves more fully as the play goes on, slowly sacrificing an unvexed sympathy we might feel for them as women making common cause with a wounded, betrayed sister. Consider, for instance, when Medea, ignoring their pleas, goes into her house, resolved to murder her children. What do the Chorus say in response to this impending crime? They talk about the luck of those who never had children, how much trouble child-rearing is, how uncertain its outcome, and so on and so forth. Here I am, their translator, more than a little aghast, expecting floods of outrage and sorrow at the deed Medea is about to do. And what I find instead is a weird paean to the blessings of the barren, who will never know the burdens of raising ungrateful, unemployable, or, should they turn out well, mortal children.

What kind of poorly disguised identification is going on between these women and the one about to butcher her young? Even to us post-moderns schooled in the acceptance of ambivalence, this response is wrenching in its inappropriateness to the extremity of the situation, making the Chorus callous and obliquely complicit. And when the messenger recounts in graphic, sickening detail the atrocious death of the young princess and the old king, "a sight," he says, "to wring tears from a stone," the only response of the dry-eyed Chorus is to ignore the victims and say, self-righteously, that Jason has deserved these disasters.

The uneasiness about their stance is brought by Euripides to an acute edge when, during those terrible moments when the children are actually being killed and cry out for help, he has the Chorus protest that they should not allow this to continue; they seem about to intervene—and then, as if they were in a Beckett play, they do absolutely nothing. They are paralyzed all but linguistically—as if the rift between word and deed has become an acknowledged and visible chasm, and shame has fled the earth, as the Chorus had said of Jason's perfidy in an earlier ode when their pious eloquence was still convincing:

> The sacred oath, its power,
> is overthrown,
> and shame from Hellas flown—
> she has taken wing for high Olympus,
> where she hides her face in cloud.

Many of Medea's speeches are righteous, too, often genuinely so, as if constantly to remind us that the best causes can have the worst representatives or succumb to vile actions, and that to wound people is not to make them the great human beings our sympathies for the injustices done to them would have them be, but rather to damage them and make them vengeful. That the most ardent and articulate statement in the Classical tradition of the evils to which a woman's lot subjects her comes from the mouth of a figure who has already committed abhorrent acts (including the murder of her own brother to forward her lover's ambitions) and will soon commit worse ones, is to undermine any moral clarity that could be put to political uses. By making Medea the murderer of her own children, which scholarly consensus now considers Euripides' original alteration of the accepted version (in which the Corinthians killed the children to avenge the murder of their ruling family), he not only turns tragic action to horror show but makes finally impossible any sense of Medea's moral agency.

Equally in her passion, her intelligence, her pride, her powers, her ability to bend others to her will, her blood relationship to a god, her ruthless determination to destroy her enemies, her refusal ever to play the victim, Medea embodies qualities admired in the male ruler or hero, and her appropriation of those qualities in the play ironically shows them for what they most brutally are. (In the same way as seeing a man play Desdemona to a female Othello made emphatically clear just how weak and simpering was the part that had heretofore seemed so admirably loving.)

Medea makes this double standard explicit in a soliloquy which she ends with these words:

> . . . Take heart, Medea,
> use all your arts, inquire of all you know, and all you are—
> spare nothing. For what they did to you—those sons
> of double-dealing, false-speaking Sisyphus—foul murder
> is a fair return. Have the courage of your kind: the seed
> of gods spawned you—the offspring of a noble father, and Helios,
> the sun himself, your grandsire. Fire is your element;
> you know what you must do. Well, we are women, aren't we,
> our best designs have made us architects of harm, for deeds
> of glory are denied to us—so we must do our worst.

That her worst, when mounted and armored and *his*, is traditionally called glorious is one of the great unmasking truths of this play. The anger of Achilles has a different playing field from the anger of Medea, and Euripides seems guided here by a gaunter muse than Homer or his descendants, producing an art in which truth is far from coincident with beauty, and the Grecian urn is filled with ashes. To complete the inversion of types, Euripides portrays the Ur-Greek hero Jason as a shallow, opportunistic, and self-deluded cad, who owes his hero's reputation—as Medea rightfully reminds him—to her wiles and powers, rather than to his own strength.

Both the one large and the many small figures seem designed to unmask the heroic, and to confront the audience with the pettiness, vanity, hypocrisy, selfishness, violence and impotent rationality of humankind, a small-ness magnified by high position. The one large and towering figure whose perverse use of her own powers and her ability to strip the self-glorifying masks from others (which becomes most horrifyingly literal in the burning off of the beauty of Jason's princess-bride by playing on her vanity) makes Medea's very magnificence, its heroism if you will, a mockery of the vileness of her means to assert her superior power, and the littleness to which such towering passion and pride will stoop. As if to measure the loss of Greek balance, disproportion is everywhere.

I was struck, as I translated, by the petty domestic squabbling of Jason and Medea, a point-scoring contest that is resumed even in the final scene over the bodies of their children. Here Euripides seemed intent on showing the dialogue form reduced to mere bickering, degrading the form which Greek philosophy and political debate brought to a high pitch. Equally striking are the relentless egoism and manipulative intent of Medea's argu-ments, so that her justly famous speech about women's lot is spoken to win the Corinthian women to her side and to bind them to secrecy, even as her brilliant unmasking of the rhetorical sophistries of rationalizing, specious argument in relation to Jason seems equally to be a smokescreen for her own more adroit use of such logical tricks.

Both Creon and especially Jason she manipulates with wheedling and flattery that are so uncharacteristic as to send off warnings to all but the most self-deluded; Aegeus of Athens, too, she plays like a lyre to her own desire's tune. And the speech in which she hesitates at the brink of child-murder and supposedly bares a mother's tender heart is itself almost com-pletely self-absorbed. She thinks not of what she is taking from her children but of what she will lose, all the mother's prerogatives she will be abdicating, and, in a stunning flight of self-pity, she imagines herself in old age, newly dead, her children lovingly washing her body in a tender finale which she will be denying herself by killing them.

This nihilistic play—its glories of eloquence and insight calculated, like the speeches of Medea that twist her listeners to her purposes, to set us up for the cruelty of disillusion, moral disproportion, and disappointed expec-tation of order—is the one which the times and the task of translation re-vealed to me. The Chorus' epilogue itself reinforces this reading, and, with a final ironic reversion to piety, attributes the outcome to Zeus. Indeed, it is the dragon chariot of her grandfather Helios, the Sun, that carries Medea triumphantly off over the heads of the Corinthians—another slaughter of the innocents underwritten by the gods, a divine sanction unacceptable to the reverent critics. What could Euripides have meant? they have asked repeatedly. Surely this must be regarded as a failure of dramatic art, this *deus ex machina* a clumsy device. But what if the ending is entirely consistent with the play's central intentions? In the process of translation, watching the play's cruel actions erase their own extenuation, the question again arose— if the pieties of the critics but drape this anatomizing of cold rage in the face of pettiness and betrayal, to what does this play owe its longevity, and even, in relation to the other Classical Greek tragedies, its exceptional and enduring popularity?

The answer to that, though it can be neither single nor simple, attests perhaps to certain unpalatable truths about ourselves (more overt and inescapable at certain places and times than others), truths which Euripides both appeals to and enacts in *Medea*. In this, our century of atrocities—of mass murder on an unprecedented and emotionally numbing scale—one truth is undeniable: that the worst sometimes overtakes the best in people, and that insanely murderous and ultimately self-ruinous "solutions" may be chosen over saner ones, even when we know better. Medea articulates this in these despairing lines: "rage will bite through reason's curb—how useless to know / that the worst harm comes to us from heedless wrath."

As translator/poet, I have, here and elsewhere, added metaphor to more fully embody and thereby evoke meaning; here I have given rage teeth, as, throughout the play, Medea—fury personified—is likened (first by the Nurse who knows her best) to a wild animal, a likeness that disorders expectation further, for the savagery of the lioness is at its pitch precisely in defense of her cubs. Medea is no force of nature but a ruthless and sophisticated individual who at once disorders both natural and civil orders as they conjoin to betray her—the first through her misplaced passion for Jason, when, in Colchis, she helped him steal the golden fleece; the second the city-state, which not only failed to protect her but, for the convenience of its rulers and out of fear of her reprisals, exiles her, expelling her like a foreign object from the body politic. In her experience—and she has been on both sides of this—passion overthrows loyalty, and hallowed law serves the caprice and ambition of the powerful.

And, over all, hangs the red spider of revenge, whose bite is deadly and whose web catches the audience from the start. What is wrong with Hamlet, he asks himself and others have asked for the centuries since, that he failed to take his revenge? Revenge is a passion that few question: if legal history is an indication, revenge predates the notion of justice and later continues, at least in the insulted heart, and often in the world at large, to preempt it. And here is Medea—used, betrayed, rejected, humiliated—who becomes the ultimate avenger, imagined for each of us, perhaps (and, who knows, perhaps for Euripides as well), the one who both dares and has the skill to torment and destroy her enemies. How many have dreamed of that satisfaction? Or better, how many have not? As a woman student candidly expressed it years ago on an exam: "I know that Medea is supposed to be a monster, but I shall always adore her."

Normally, however, the veil of morality covers the brutality of vengeance. In the *Inferno* the imagination of the exiled Dante stages an ingenious profusion of tortures, often cruel and sadistic in the extreme, but because the ethical equation of punishment-fits-the-crime has been set up as divinely (or demonically) sanctioned, even though we no longer even recognize these people without the aid of footnotes, we believe in their crimes on the evidence of the torture, and of the torturer. An odd business, really. The other way in which literature allows us to share imaginatively in the sweet pleasure of revenge is exemplified in popular work like that of Stephen King, whose plots offer the satisfaction of horrifying revenge enacted by a heretofore victimized individual, sometimes (as in *Carrie*) with the aid of special magic powers of destruction. The normal order is inevitably reinstated in these stories, but not before magic has broken the usual rules of power and we have vicariously experienced both the terrible humiliation and the even more terrible revenge of a central character.

The perennial excited interest in hellish vengeance runs through much popular work, both the enduring and the ephemeral; what sets *Medea* apart from all these revenge tales is that Euripides strips away the justifying veil. Medea's character and actions make it impossible for us to enjoy the pleasure of revenge with the impunity that the moral cover of an innocent avenger gives, or with that return to the fold when subsequent punishment of the enraged avenger puts us finally back on the side of social order. Medea is desperate, implacable, and entirely without compunction, and she succeeds. We are left to face our fascination with her malign power, or our horror at its success, and to face without consolation the atrocious acts that people, when the usual restraints fall away, are capable of committing, or at least of passively watching, as the Chorus of "good" Corinthian women look on, their protesting words mere bubbles of pious sound that burst against the walls of their inertia in the face of evil. And the complicity of the on-stage audience does raise questions about that other audience, over two millennia old now, of which we are part.

In this maelstrom of passionate disproportion, this bloody revenge played out in the bright glare of the Greek sun, awareness without pity or mitigation, I steadied myself, as I believe its original author did, with the measured cadences of poetry. Though I sought a varied diction to reflect the disparity in complexity and consciousness of the main characters, I cast all their speeches in hexameters, and those of the Chorus mainly in dimeter and trimeter, with large if not compulsive amounts of both end and internal rhyming in the choral odes. I was following in this both my own inclinations and, roughly, the example of the Greek.

I have added, as the poet resident in this text for nearly a year, what images and metaphors I thought would help enliven the speeches and enhance meaning for a contemporary English speaking audience, and have, everywhere, thought of the lines as dramatic utterances to be spoken aloud, lines of poetic dialogue that must live on the tongue and in the ear. Occasionally I have inserted, quietly so as not to disturb the dramatic and narrative flow, bits of essential background which a present day reader might otherwise have to look for in a footnote.

I know but scanty demotic Greek, and pretend to no knowledge of the Classical Greek; from many visits to Greece, the sounds of the spoken language are familiar. My consultant for the Classical Greek text, for the scholarly background, and for many of the nuances of meaning was Professor Inés Azar, Director of the Ph.D. Program in the Human Sciences, George Washington University, Washington, D.C. She is in no way, however, responsible for errors, questionable interpretive shadings, departures from the original for what I conceived to be poetic necessities. Whatever this translation lacks in either faithfulness or finesse, these shortcomings or excesses I claim as my own, with a shamelessness that is perhaps my best qualification as *Medea*'s translator in 1997.

Cast

NURSE of Medea
TUTOR to Medea's children
CHILDREN of Medea and Jason
MEDEA
CHORUS of Corinthian women
CREON, king of Corinth
JASON, Medea's husband
AEGEUS, king of Athens
MESSENGER
NONSPEAKING
  Guards
  Servant

(The action of the play takes place in the Greek city-state of Corinth, in front of the house of Medea. The Nurse enters from the house.)

NURSE

If only the Argo had never spread its sails and flown
across the waves to distant Colchis, passing through
the dark Symplegades, those clashing rocks that lock
the blue straits to the East. If only the forest of pine
had not been felled to build the ship and hew the oars
that took the heroes to that foreign place. If only Jason
and his men had not been sent by the command of Pelias
the king, to seek the serpent-guarded Golden Fleece.
For then Medea, my mistress, would not have taken ship
for high-walled Iolchus, her heart clawed by love   10
for Jason. And she would not have tricked the daughters
of king Pelias into killing him, would not have made
her home with Jason and their children here in Corinth, cut off
forever from the country and the cradle of her birth.

At first, though, her life here was fortunate—with husband,
children, and the sympathy of the Corinthians
for the exile in their midst. To share everything with Jason
was her happiness. Life is an untroubled sea when
what a woman wants agrees with what her husband seeks.

But now the waters of content are roiled, all is hostile   20
to Medea, love is her enemy, and all that she holds dear
is sick. For Jason has deserted both his children and his wife,
and made his bed on royal sheets: he has wed the daughter
of Creon, Corinth's king.
                          Medea burns with shame.
Dishonored, she calls out to the gods to witness his betrayal,
invokes that vow he swore with his own right hand;
cast aside, she cries aloud what she has given him,
and how he serves her in return. Since she learned of his
                          desertion,
food has not passed her lips, she gives herself entirely up
to a terrible despair, cries out, and melts time into tears.   30
Lost in pain, she will not raise her eyes nor lift
her face from the ground.
                          As well to move a stone, or turn
the waves back with a word, as to reach her. She speaks to
                          no one,
but to herself she weeps and murmurs of her beloved father,
her lost country and her kin, of all that she betrayed for him
who now dishonors her. Her own torn heart bears witness
now to what she did when she abandoned home.

And her children—she draws back at the sight of them.
I fear what dreadful plans she may conceal; the iron
weight of wrath is far too great to be endured within.   40
I fear that even now she hones the sword, and means
herself to drive it through her rival's belly as she lies
on the bridal bed, or kill the king, and Jason, all—
and leave a trail of blood in the wake of her insulted

pride. She is formidable. No one who crosses her
can hope to greet the morning light victorious, and crow.

But look. Here come her boys, home from their games,
                untroubled
by their mother's griefs. That is the way with the young—
to them, grief is no more than a passing cloud.
(Enter Tutor with the two children of Medea and Jason.)

TUTOR

    Aged slave, nurse and servant to the house, what are   50
    you doing out here, lamenting to yourself? What is the good
    of pouring misery back into your own ears?
    Does Medea, our mistress, wish to be left entirely alone?

NURSE

    Old Tutor, long time attendant to Lord Jason's sons, you know
    how the loyal servant's heart is pierced when the master's luck
    runs out on a bad roll of the dice. Overcome with grief,
    I had to come out here to tell my lady's sorrows to the only
    audience I have: the silent earth, the empty sky.

TUTOR

    Is she still inconsolable? Not yet resigned?

NURSE

    I wish I shared your happy ignorance. Her pain has just   60
    begun its climb—like a building wave, it has not reached
    that peak where it will break, and crash.

TUTOR

    Poor fool (though I tempt the gods to speak of my betters
    so), it is our mistress who is the ignorant one, old nurse;
    she doesn't know that worse news follows bad.

NURSE

    Tell me, old man. Don't leave me in suspense.

TUTOR

It's nothing. I have said more than I should.

NURSE

By your beard I beg you, and as your fellow slave,
I beg you—tell me. If it is a secret, I will keep it close.

TUTOR

It is something that I overheard the old men say, the ones   70
who sit at the gaming tables near the holy Pierian spring.
Pretending not to listen, I heard one say that Creon,
Corinth's king, was going to exile these two children
and their mother from our land. I don't know if the tale
is true or no, but I fear it may be so.

NURSE

That he is through with her, I understand; but will Jason
let them cast his own sons out like so much trash?

TUTOR

Old marriage bonds become an inconvenience when a man
moves on. I fear that Jason will no longer shield this house.

NURSE

We have not passed through one storm and another breaks.   80
Too soon—I hear the very timbers groan; our ruin is sure.

TUTOR

Tell no one of this news I overheard. Your mistress must
                              not know.

NURSE

Children, do you hear how little your father cares for you?
I curse him—no, what am I saying? He is my master. And yet,
how be loyal to one who shows no loyalty to his own?

TUTOR

    Well, he is only human, after all. He has
    a new and royal bride; these boys are in his way.
    Don't you know by now that men put self-love first?

NURSE

    Now boys, go on inside. It's going to be all right. And you,
    keep them far away from their mother in her rage; I have seen   90
    her turn a savage look their way, and my heart quailed.
    She will keep her anger chained until, a tiger, she turns
    it loose unfed. Then pray it is her enemies
    on whom it feeds, and not on those she loves.

MEDEA *(within)*

    Ay! Despised, cast out, sick with sorrow,
    most miserable of women, I! Aaaay! If only I could die!

NURSE

    As I told you, dear ones, your mother whips her grief-tormented
    heart into a fury. Go quickly into the house and stay out
    of her sight. Don't come near her now. She baits her anger
    with a prod. Beware her raging sorrow and her savage ways!   100
    Quick—get inside now, fast as you can.
(Exit Tutor and children into the house.)
    Laments and wailing rise from her, like smoke from a burning
    house. And when fresh injury pours oil on the fire,
    I fear the flames from the furnace of her sorrow-blasted
    soul will sear us all. What won't she do?

MEDEA *(within)*

    Aiee! Unhappy as I am, I can suffer this no more!
    The bitterest lament cannot contain the measure of my grief.
    Oh children of a hateful mother, cursed by your very birth,
    may you perish with your father, may this house fall into
    ruin, may its dust be swept into the bin by slaves!   110

NURSE

> Ay! Ay me! The father's is the sin. Why must the children
> share the blame? Why would you hate them? Oh children, I fear
> for you; blank terror stalks my heart. For those with power
> are dangerous: used to being obeyed, nothing checks
> their willfulness. They swing from mood to mood, loose
> cargo in a stormy hold. Let me grow old, secure and
> unassuming, used to no more than my share; the middle way
> is best, and keeps life on an even keel. Riches in excess
> and lordly privilege aren't meant for mortals—no. When
> the gods
> fall on those who have the most, they pick them to the bones.   120

(Chorus enters.)

CHORUS

> It was her voice,
> her cry, the wretched
> woman of Colchis—
> again I heard it. Is she still
> not calm? Is there no balm
> to soothe her? Old
> woman, tell me the truth.
> Even inside my double-gated
> house I heard those chants
> of lamentation;   130
> I heard her cry—
> but of what wrongs?
> I can take no pleasure
> in the misfortune
> of this house, for I have shared
> the cup of friendship there.

NURSE

> The house is no more than a shell. Its former lord has gone
> to a royal marriage bed. Cast away, his one-time wife,
> my mistress, keeps fast in her room, and lengthens time
> with tears

and dreadful cries, and will take no comfort in the words
of friends.   140

MEDEA *(within)*

Aiee! May a bolt of lightning strike me dead!
Why should I drag myself, a broken-legged thing,
through empty days? If death would come for me,
and free me of my hateful life, then—oh, sweet rest!

CHORUS

O Zeus, and fruitful Earth,
and lucid Sun,
attend! Did you hear
this young wife's wail
of pain?
     But you, foolish
woman—why desire   150
to sleep with Death?
That bed awaits us
all too soon—
what folly to invite it
out of time. And as to
husbands who desert
their wives to wed
their own advantage, Zeus
will settle that score.
Your husband does not   160
deserve your tears;
your grief by far
exceeds his worth.

MEDEA

O mighty Themis who sets the balance right,
and night-ruling Artemis, hear me! Do you see how
I am wronged, tied by firm oaths to an accursed husband.
May I live to see him and his new bride—her royal
house and train—ground into grit as fine as meal

fit to feed pigs, for they have wronged me without cause,
I who was never their foe.

       O father, O city of my birth,   170
I feel my shame—to help Jason live, I killed my brother.

NURSE

Do you hear her prayers, how she calls on Zeus' daughter,
Themis, guardian of oaths, avenger of men's broken vows?
Imperious, these prayers—no small revenge will do. Who knows
what she will undertake before this rage is spent?

CHORUS

If only she would come outside
and let us meet her—face to face;
perhaps our words could turn
her anger's tide, perhaps
we could, if not erase,   180
at least assuage her rage,
avert what rises from her heart.
May our good will never fail
our friends. Go now
and coax her from the house;
tell her that friends are here;
go quick, we fear her harm
to those inside. Like an army
that has begun its charge,
her grief is driving forward   190
toward its cause.

NURSE

I will try. Though I am doubtful I can pry her
from the fastness of her pride. Still, I will serve you, and
persuade her if I can—though she growls and glowers
like a lioness with cubs at any servant who comes close
and tries to speak.

      Would that there were songs to tame
the bitterness of mortal woe: for its relief wars are begun,

great houses ruined, the floodgates of violence opened.
Orpheus, though he could soften the hearts of beasts
and gods, had no song to quiet the furies of human grief.   200
Like him, our bards of old were helpless in the face
of rage; their harmonies were made to play at banquets
and at festivals where happiness abounds, where
the cakes are soaked in honey, and song's redundant.
Would that sweet music were devised—and wiser men
would tune the lyres in that more necessary key—
to mend the wounded heart, and make of lyric arts
a healing balm.
(Exit Nurse into the house.)

CHORUS

We heard the tortured
music of her cries,   210
how she calls for him
whom she despises now—
Jason: traitor, breaker
of vows, defiler of
their marriage bed.
We heard her call
on Themis, Goddess
of Oaths, daughter
of Olympic Zeus;
Themis, who   220
gives weight to the words
of men. By her good
faith, Medea came
to Hellas across the sea,
braved the swallowing
salt darkness; sailed
through the narrow straits
of the Black Sea,
passing where
few have gone.   230
(Medea and Nurse enter from the house.)

MEDEA

Women of Corinth, you have summoned me, and I have
come. I would not have your ill report. How easy it is
to be mistaken by the world, I know. Though there are
many who are arrogant, who do not hesitate—whether in
the open marketplace or behind their walls—to lord it over
all, yet there are those who live a quiet life, who shun
publicity, and, for diffidence and sweet reserve, they get
a reputation for indifference, for thinking themselves above
the common lot. Justice is not in the eyes of men:
judgment runs before knowledge. Before a man's true   240
character is known, people believe the worst; they hate
so easily and on the least of grounds—though the man
has done them not the slightest wrong. Above all,
a foreigner must not resist the general will, but be
compliant with the city's wish—though I do not mean
to praise or to excuse the citizen who is self-willed
and lacks civility. But in my case, a blow as if
from nowhere struck me down. I am destroyed: my joy
in life is done. I have but one desire: I want to die.
For he to whom my life and all were bound, has proved   250
the worst of men. And now disgrace is all I own.
Of all the sentient creatures of the earth, we women are
the most unfortunate. First there is the dowry: at such
exorbitant expense we have to buy a husband—pay
to take a master for our bodies. And as the seasons pass,
if he prove false, then are we twice abused. For our initial
loss (which custom celebrates) is multiplied beyond
the estimation of a cost: it is our pride that is insulted,
trampled underfoot. All our hopes and striving lean
on this one thing: whether the husband that we take   260
turns out good or ill. For marriage is the only choice
we have, and divorce discredits women utterly.
We leave the house we knew, the dear comfort of familiar
ways. We must enter the husband's world, accommodate
strange practices, the habits of his house, and figure out—

oh, hardest yet—how best to deal with his whims, for little
in our past prepares us for this task of satisfying him.
If after all our work to break our own will on the wheel
of his, and, with studied art, to mate desire with necessity—
if then the man has still not tired of us, does not resent   270
the marriage yoke: then, in the sorority of wives,
our lives are enviable.
                    Otherwise, one is better off dead.
A man when he is bored at home, or irritated by
the burdens of domestic life, goes out into the streets,
or to the baths, debates philosophy for sport, diverts
himself with games and friends, and does what pleases him.
Our lives are monotone: for on one man we're forced
to fix our gaze. Men say we lead an easy life,
safe at home while they risk all at the point of a spear.
What do they know? I would rather stand three times   280
in battle with shield and spear than give birth once.

But though we share a woman's lot, your story and mine
diverge. You have a city and the sanctuary of a father's
house, you yet enjoy your life and bask in the warmth
and company of friends. While I, bereft of city and of kin,
am by my husband's outrage left exposed—unwanted
as a child left on a hill to the vultures and the quarreling dogs.
For I was booty carried from a foreign land, orphaned
by distance; I have no mother, no brother, no family to offer
refuge from the wreckage of my hopes. So I ask you one favor.   290
If I find means and opportunity to punish my faithless
husband—sisters, keep my secret. For though a woman
turn away at the sight of the blood-drenched field of war,
and shudder at the cold steel blade—when she is scorned in love,
no warrior, however fierce, has thoughts as murderous as hers.

CHORUS LEADER

I will keep your secret, Medea. Your cause is just, for you
are wronged. Your husband must be punished. I understand

your grief, and that it seeks relief, as streams flow down,
tearing aside whatever rocks may block their way.

But here comes Creon, and, in the way of kings, no doubt   300
he comes to bring some new edict. What can it be?
(Enter Creon with his guards.)

CREON

You, Medea, who disturb our peace with rage against
your husband—I order you to leave this land at once,
go into exile, and your children with you. At once, I say—
for this decree is mine, and I will see you gone myself,
outside the borders of this land, before I go back home.

MEDEA

Aiee! I am utterly destroyed! My enemies come full sail—
from the narrowing straits of blind misfortune, I can see no
                    escape.
Is not my suffering unendurable enough? I ask you: why?
Creon, I ask you why you wish to banish me.   310

CREON

Well, I see no reason at all to hide the fact
that I'm afraid for my daughter, of what you might
do to her, what deadly harm, as you have all
the means—your cleverness, your skill in evil arts,
and certainly the record shows what you can do.
Stung by the loss of your husband's marriage bed, you dare
threaten to harm the bride, her husband—even me!
This is the report that many bring—well, *an ounce
of prevention,* and so on . . . better that you should hate me now,
than I be soft, and live to repent it later.   320

MEDEA

Ah, Creon. This is not the first time that my reputation
hurt me, and led others to misjudge my honest aims.
A sensible man should not educate his children too much,

make them too wise, for their learning will earn them little more
than the malice of their fellows, who will accuse them
of everything malign—idleness, intrigue, whatever their envy
can invent. If you bring new ideas to fools, they will hate
you for it; whatever they fail to understand, they judge
as useless, or worse. And if your reputation outstrips
those whom the city acknowledges as its most clever men,   330
then you become an irritation—a thorn in order's tender skin.
I share this fate I speak of—my cleverness and education
have brought me the enmity of some, by others I am thought
withdrawn, or else too forward, too formidable—and yet,
my wisdom is but small, I cannot raise an army, or a wind,
I have no power—and still you fear me. What harm could I
do you? Creon, have no fear of me; I am no criminal to plot
against my rulers. What reason would I have? You have done
me no injustice. It is my husband that I hate, not you, nor
your good fortune. You married your daughter to the man   340
on whom your own heart placed the seal. A choice sincere,
and sensible; you acted well. May the marriage, may you all
prosper in the days ahead. Only let me stay here in Corinth.
For, though I am wronged, I am not wroth—I put aside
           complaint,
and I will be compliant now, and yield to my superiors.

CREON

Your words are soothing to my ear, but I dare not trust them.
I fear you only feign; beneath these yielding words,
deep in your heart, you plot to harm us. Your honeyed words
have only added force to what I first suspected.
It is easier to protect oneself against a woman in a passion—   350
or a man for that matter—than one wise enough to keep
her own counsel. No more argument: go at once into exile—
my decree is fixed; no enemy of mine remains in Corinth.

MEDEA

Oh, no. I beg you by your knees and by your newly wedded
           daughter!

CREON

It is no use; I can't be won. Woman, you waste your words.

MEDEA

But will you banish me and so refuse a suppliant?

CREON

Yes. Should I put you before the love I owe my own?

MEDEA

Oh fatherland! Now my thoughts are filled with you.

CREON

And mine. Next to my children, my land is nearest to my heart.

MEDEA

Oh, what a curse is love!

CREON

                                        Well, it all depends.   360

MEDEA

Zeus, mark well who is responsible for all this grief!

CREON

Plague take you, woman—go! And rid me of this burden.

MEDEA

The suffering is mine. I have no need of more.

CREON

In a minute, my servants will throw you out by force.

MEDEA

No, no. Oh please, I beg you, Creon, not yet.

CREON

Woman, you are like a fly buzzing in my ear.

MEDEA

    Your banishment I accept. It is not from that I sought reprieve.

CREON

    Infuriating woman, what then? Why still cling to my hand,
    using a suppliant's sacred claim to bend my will?

MEDEA

    I ask for but one day, today, to make provision   370
    for exile, for my children, whom their father abandons.
    But you, a parent too, will naturally have pity on them;
    you will be shepherd to my lambs. For myself, I care nothing;
    exile for me is neither here nor there. It is for my children
    that I sorrow, for their departure I would prepare the way.

CREON

    I have not the cast of mind to play the tyrant's role,
    though I have paid, and dearly so, for clemency.
    I know to grant your plea is a grave mistake, and yet
    I grant it. But if tomorrow's sun should find you and
    your sons within this land, then, straight away, you will   380
    be put to death. My word on this is final. Stay then
    for this last day. Too little time to do the harm I feared.
(Exit Creon and guards.)

CHORUS

    Unhappy woman, woe!
    Crushed by misfortune
    from every side,
    spurned as you are,
    where can you turn?
    What house or land
    will unlock its gates
    to let a stranger in?   390
    From such calamity,
    none can set you

free. A god has cast
you, Medea, into
misfortune's sea
with no way out.

MEDEA

Who would deny that things look bad? But don't think
that weaker hands can shape my end—for it is I who have
transforming power in my arts. The newlyweds will
struggle in my wiles, and I will catch as well the maker   400
of the match. Do you think I would have fawned on such
a man unless I stood to gain, unless it served my plan?
I would not have deigned to speak to him, much less to touch
him with entreating hands. What a fool he is! He had it in
his power to banish me and thwart my plans; instead
he gave me what I asked: this day, the time to turn them
into corpses—father, daughter, husband—on a single pyre.
I have so many ways to kill them; my friends, I hardly know
which one to try out first. Shall I set fire to the bridal chamber,
or impale them on a sword—or both, and roast them like kids   410
on a spit? But though the prospect warms my blood, yet
something gives me pause—if I am caught inside their house,
an uninvited guest entering the hated chamber where lies
the bridal bed, I will be killed instead, my enemies rejoice.
The better choice is the certain means, the skill I know:
poison—and take their lives without endangering mine.
But, wait. Why save a life that no one will protect? Suppose that
I succeed—what city will receive me? What stranger will
                    reach out
a hand? What land will offer sanctuary? What house awaits me?
There is none. So I will abide a little while, and if some
                    stronghold   420
appears to shelter me, then the murder shall be done by stealth.
But if the gates of hope are closed to me, then I shall take
the sword and, daring all, hack my way to my revenge, and die
for it. By Her whom I worship first and last, the goddess Hecate,
who lives in the inmost chamber of my house, and of my bowels,

none of them shall cause me pain and live to smile at it. Bitter
shall I make this vile marriage, and bitter Creon who thought
to build his power on the ruins of mine. Take heart, Medea,
use all your arts, inquire of all you know, and all you are—
spare nothing. For what they did to you—those sons   430
of double-dealing, false-speaking Sisyphus—foul murder
is a fair return. Have the courage of your kind: the seed
of gods spawned you—the offspring of a noble father,
      and Helios,
the sun himself, your grandsire. Fire is your element;
you know what you must do. Well, we are women, aren't we,
our best designs have made us architects of harm, for deeds
of glory are denied to us—so we must do our worst.

CHORUS
    Backward flow the rivers,
    uphill to their source,
    justice and the order   440
    of the universe
    reversed; the god-sworn
    oaths that held men
    to their word are torn
    like rotted rope.
    Now will the feet
    of sense tread air, and
    thought stand on its head.
    Now will men admire
    our women's ways, and give   450
    us sway; no more will they
    insult and slander us; honor
    shall be our daily bread.

    No more will the poets of old
    sing of our fickleness. If Apollo,
    lord of song, had given women
    the gift to make the lyre sing
    with glorious power, why then

we would have set the ears
of men on fire with our reply.   460
No matter, in the length of days,
for men as well as us, time
will have its say: no one is safe.

But your fate moves us—you sailed
from the strong halls of your father's
land, unmoored by love, you passed
the clashing rocks, the narrow straits
from the Black Sea. Now, a stranger
on a foreign soil, you have lost all:
your marriage bed, your husband's   470
love, this borrowed land, a nest
for your little ones—an exile, driven out,
your honor gone with the rest.

The sacred oath, its power,
is overthrown,
and shame from Hellas flown—
she has taken wing for high Olympus,
where she hides her face in cloud.
To what then can you appeal—
who have no father's harbor   480
to drop your anchor in?
Ill-fated woman: a princess
rules the house, a better match
for his advantage now, she is
the mistress in your place.
(Enter Jason.)

JASON

How many times before I've seen your wrath, fierce,
ungovernable—and known it for the evil that it is—
one for which no remedy exists. You could
have kept this house and land if you had held your tongue,
you who will not patiently bear decisions made   490

by those in power. Your own rash words have forced
the king to exile you. Not that it matters to me; go on
if you want, call me every name you know, the lowest
of the low, what do I care? But as for your slander of
the ruling family—you are lucky that merely exile is
the royal decree. I did all I could for you; I tried to cool
the king's hot temper for your sake; I did not wish you
gone. But you lack all restraint; it is your folly in reviling
the ruling house that brought this exile on your head.
As for me, I honor my obligations—in spite of your abuse   500
I would not fail the ones I love; it is your interest that brings
me here, I know the hardships exile brings, and would not
have you go penniless or unprovisioned to that uncertain
state. Even if you hate me, I bear no grudge toward you.

MEDEA

You vile worm, maggot on the rotting carcass of your vows.
I call you only what your acts deserve—unmanly thing!
You dare to come with such an unctuous tone, you, worst
enemy of mine, and of the sacred ties that bind the world.
This is not brave, nor bold—to wrong your loved ones, then
look them in the face. This is the lowest action of our race: 510
shamelessness. Well, you did right to come, for now you'll
hear what I really think of you—my words will pull the arrow
from my heart, and drive it through your self-deceiving eyes.

I shall begin where it all began. I saved your life—and all
the Greeks who sailed the Argo under your command, be
my witness—when you were sent to yoke the murderous, fire-
breathing bulls and sow the field of death with dragon
teeth. It was I who killed the sleepless dragon whose coils
wrapped the tree where the Golden Fleece was hung. My magic
saved your life and made your hero's name, and lit the way   520
back from certain death. Of my own free will, I betrayed
home, father, friends, and came with you to Iolcus, threw
prudence to the wind, for love of you. I murdered its king,
Pelias, your enemy, by the worst of deaths, at the hands of

his own daughters who thought to make him young again—
poor fools, duped by my wiles. Thus his house and power
I destroyed, for love of you. And so I saved you at my own
expense, and raised you high, only to find you low,
most base of men, betrayer, opportunist, who takes a wife
more advantageous in my place. And not because you lack
                              an heir—   530
for, with all that, I have borne you children, hale and fair.

I wonder if you think the ancient gods no longer rule,
and in their stead, petty statutes are set up to prosper cads—
for you must know that you have mocked your sacred oath.
Look now at my right hand, the hand you took when you
came to my knees, a suppliant, and see it empty now,
as empty as the one who fixed his grasp on me, stole
my past and fleeced me of my hopes. Still, I'll
share my thoughts with you, as with a friend—and yet,
what good could ever come of *you*? But I will speak—   540
my questions will expose you, stripped in the glaring light
of consequence. Tell me, where can I turn now? To my
father, he whom I betrayed to bring you here? Or to the
wretched daughters of Pelias? Imagine them with open
arms to succor me who made them agents of their father's
death! To my own blood and kin I have become a deadly
foe, and all for you I have made enemies of those
I never would have harmed. And what return for this!
How happy these Greek women see me now, a paragon
of joy, how fine and faithful a husband you appear as I   550
am forced to flee, exiled, deprived of friends, abandoned
with the children you cast off like toys you had outgrown.
What a bridegroom you appear—your children wandering
the hills like beggars, and she who saved you with them,
cast away!
            O Zeus! why did you give mankind a sign
to separate with ease the true gold from the counterfeit,
and not so constitute the human form that we might know
at once the base man from the true?

CHORUS LEADER
> When friend turns on friend, and there is wrath between those
> closest joined—it is a wrath that nothing can appease.   560

JASON
> Woman, in such a storm of abuse as you have raised,
> to keep my course I must pull in my sail, run close before
> the tiresome wind of your complaint. While you exaggerate
> what you have done for me, and why—then my restraint
> shall set the record straight. It was not you but Aphrodite
> who favored me, and she, alone of gods and mortals, saved
> my expedition from defeat. It was your clever mind befriended
> me, I grant you that, and I will stop myself from mentioning
> how Eros with his arrows pinned your heart to my plans—
> I do not wish to seem petty on this point. So I will let that go,   570
> for so far as you did help me, you did well. But you did well
> for yourself, that I must add: in saving me, you got more
> than you gave. I shall enumerate how much you gained:
> first, you joined the civilized; you live among the Greeks and
> not barbarians; you have been taught what justice is, and how
> law rules in place of force. And you have gained a reputation
> for cleverness among the Greeks, a fine renown. While, if you
> lived at the end of the world, your name would be as lost
> as a diamond buried by a slide of rock. What good is gold
> or a godlike gift for drawing from the lyre a sweeter song   580
> than Orpheus himself, if one has not the grace of fame!
>
> I could not help but speak of what I've done for you—
> you are the one who started this debate. And you reproach
> me for the royal marriage I have made, so I am forced
> to demonstrate, first, how it shows me wise; second,
> self-controlled; and third, a faithful friend to my children
> and to you.
>   Wait, hold your peace. Remember how
> I came here from Iolchus, a man stalked by misfortune,
> exiled and unconnected in this land: what greater luck
> than to have made a marriage with the daughter of the king!   590

It was not that I was tired of your bed—that is the sorest
point for you, it seems—nor was it desire for a new bride
that brought me to her bed, nor did I wish to rival others
by the siring of more sons (for we have enough already;
about that I have no reason to complain)—but all my thought
was that we should live well, for all depends on that:
everyone runs when he sees a penniless friend. I wanted
to raise my children as befits my lineage, to beget brothers
to the children born to you and raise them to the same high
rank, and by drawing all my progeny into one family,   600
I would prosper. And you, what use have you for any more
children? As for me, my future children would benefit the sons
already born. Can you fault such a plan? Not even you could
find a flaw in such a prudent move, were you not so envious
in this matter of sex. You foolish women are so ruled
by your emotions that if your life goes well in bed you think
yourselves the queens of circumstance, while if things go wrong
in bed, you turn against and hate what serves your own best
interests. Mankind should find another way to propagate
its seed. Without the female sex, life would be trouble-free.   610

CHORUS LEADER

Jason, your argument's
adroit, your points
are logical, and
yet—though perhaps
it would be wise
to hold my tongue—
I feel I must say
that it still seems wrong
to abandon your wife
in quite this way.   620

MEDEA

I am different from the common run of folk who think
fine argument deserves applause. To me, the plausible

speaker is the most dangerous; he who sends false logic
to ambush truth deserves the greatest punishment. For
he, of all men, is most confident of the power of his tongue
to justify what action he will take, however base.
Yet, like you, he is not as wise as he thinks. With me,
it would be best to skip the specious arguments, and all
false posturing of rhetoric: a single point destroys your case—
if this marriage were so advantageous to us all, you would   630
have asked for my consent before you made it, and not
gone sneaking out to wed behind your family's back.

JASON

And a fine support you would have given had I brought
you this proposal before the fact; had I asked for your
approval of a marriage, which even now, being done,
has set a raging fire in your heart—a fire which neither
reason nor good counsel can persuade you to put out.

MEDEA

It wasn't that you feared my answer. You were anxious to rid
yourself of a barbarian wife, no asset to your ambitions here.

JASON

I assure you, once again, that it was not for a woman's sake   640
that I married the king's daughter, but as I have just explained,
I did it to protect you, and to beget royal brothers for my sons;
all this I did to make our house secure, and prosper it.

MEDEA

I never wished for happiness whose roots grew out of pain,
nor prosperity as a gold spike driven through my heart.

JASON

Can you not school yourself in wisdom and change your plea?
Pray that you never more will see advantage as a source of pain,
nor think yourself in misery when fortune smiles your way.

MEDEA

Cheap words. For you have refuge here, while I go
friendless into exile, desolate, alone, bereft of place.   650

JASON

That is your choice. Blame no one but yourself.

MEDEA

No one at all? Did I take another wife and abandon you?

JASON

You uttered those unholy curses against the royal family.

MEDEA

And just by being here, I am a curse to your house, too.

JASON

I shall argue with you no further. Still, if you wish to get money
from me to help the children and yourself in exile, you have only
to ask for what you need. I am ready to give with an open hand,
and I will give you tokens to my friends, who can shelter you.
Only a fool would refuse this offer. Woman, let your anger go.

MEDEA

Accept help from your friends? Never. And I will take nothing   660
from you. One is soiled by taking offerings from a dirty hand.

JASON

The gods be my witness that I am still willing to give you
and the children what I can. But you refuse what is good
for you; with arrogance you turn away your own
best friends. By this, you only suffer more.

MEDEA

Go on: you must yourself be suffering from desire—you've been
so long away from the palace, and from the arms of your
new bride. Go, play the panting bridegroom! I smile

to think of you married so well, for perhaps—if the gods
have willed it so—this match of yours will light a pyre,   670
and all your tears will not suffice to put the fire out.
(Exit Jason.)

CHORUS
Love in excess
brings no good
in its train, but
only pain, and
a good name
lost. If Aphrodite
comes with modest
gifts, then, bless her
as the bringer   680
of a gracious
happiness.
O Goddess, never
may you smear
your unerring
arrow with
the fatal honey
of obsessive
desire, nor let it fly
from the gold string   690
of your bow
into my defenseless
heart.
     May moderation
be my lot—of all the gifts
the gods bestow, most
beautiful. May Aphrodite
spare me from
the hateful storms,
the spiteful quarreling
of passion spurned;   700
may she who rules the heart

never make mine burn
with desire
for a stranger's bed.
May she direct us wisely
when we are to wed,
and honor
a peaceful match,
a steadfast pair.

O fatherland, O house   710
of mine, may I never
be without you, outside
my city-state, never
have to wander helpless
from place to place,
the cruelest fate,
most to be pitied.
May death, yes even
death take me down, and
light with me, rather than   720
be un-citied,
lose my native land.
Of all our mortal sorrows,
the worst is
loss of place.

This is not hearsay,
but the witness of our eyes;
how everything turns away
from the one cast out,
the suffering one for whom   730
the heart should ache:
no city will open its gates,
friends disappear, no one
will reach out a hand.
But I say: let the man die
unloved who will not stand

firm for his friends, who
will not open his doors
and honor his word
to one in need. Such a man   740
I never would call friend.
(Enter Aegeus.)

AEGEUS

Medea, I wish you joy—
what better word than that to greet a friend.

MEDEA

Joy to you as well, Aegeus, son of wise Pandion!
Where have you been that brings you to this land?

AEGEUS

I have come from Phoebus Apollo's ancient oracle.

MEDEA

What took you to his Sibyl, the earth's prophetic mouth?

AEGEUS

I went to inquire how I might beget children.

MEDEA

By the gods, have you lived so long without children?

AEGEUS

I am childless, Medea, by some god's inscrutable design.   750

MEDEA

Have you a wife, or have you, as a king, preferred to stay
aloof from marriage bonds and kept yourself apart?

AEGEUS

Not at all. I have a wife who shares my name and bed.

MEDEA

What did Phoebus then reveal about your childlessness?

AEGEUS

    Words too wise, too deep, for mortals to make out.

MEDEA

    Does the law permit your telling what the oracle pronounced?

AEGEUS

    It does, of course. I seek now for a wise mind to decipher it.

MEDEA

    If it is lawful to speak, tell me what the god prophesied.

AEGEUS

    "Do not untie the wineskin's long, extended spout . . . "

MEDEA

    Until you do what? Or until you arrive at what place?   760

AEGEUS

    " . . . until you find yourself at hearth and home again."

MEDEA

    So, then, what caused you to shift course and sail this way?

AEGEUS

    I seek the man named Pittheus, king of Troezen.

MEDEA

    Ah yes, the son of Pelops, praised as a man most pious.

AEGEUS

    It is with him I wish to share this riddling oracle.

MEDEA

    The man has much experience in this, and he is wise.

AEGEUS

    Fortunate indeed that, of all my allies, he is the closest.

MEDEA

Well, all good luck to you, may you get what you desire!

AEGEUS

But I see now the tracks of tears along your cheeks,
the marks of some strong grief. What is the cause of this?   770

MEDEA

Aegeus, my husband, of all men, is the most cruel.

AEGEUS

What do you mean? Be clear and tell me what afflicts you.

MEDEA

Jason injures me, though I have never done him any harm.

AEGEUS

What has he done? Be frank and clear with me.

MEDEA

He has made another woman mistress of our house.

AEGEUS

Can it be true that he has dared to act so shamefully?

MEDEA

True indeed. He loved me once, but now dishonors me.

AEGEUS

Did some passion take his reason, or did he tire of your bed?

MEDEA

A great passion has made him unfaithful to his family.

AEGEUS

Let him go then, since, as you say, he is beneath contempt.   780

MEDEA

But he aimed high: his passion was to wed a king's daughter.

AEGEUS

Who has given his daughter to him? Tell me more.

MEDEA

Creon, king of Corinth, ruler of this very land.

AEGEUS

Now it is clear to me why he has injured you.

MEDEA

Alas, I am lost! What is more, I am exiled from this land.

AEGEUS

By whom? One misfortune follows another as you speak.

MEDEA

It is King Creon himself who exiles me from Corinth.

AEGEUS

And Jason? How could he consent to such a thing?

MEDEA

Though his words may protest, in fact, he goes along.

Now, I beg you, Aegeus, by your beard and by your knees,   790
as the gods rule, I make myself your suppliant: have pity,
pity on a helpless woman; don't let them exile me without
a friend, but say you will receive me, a suppliant to your land
and to your house. May you grant my request, and may
the gods grant yours: may your longing for children be
fulfilled, and may you, full of years, assured of heirs,
die happy. You do not know what lucky chance has thrown
me in your path. For I will make the barren tree blossom:
you shall beget children. I know the potions to make it so.

AEGEUS

    Dear woman, how many reasons argue for the granting   800
    of your plea: first, for the sacred gods, then for the children
    you promise I shall have. There I am desperate for a remedy.
    My answer is this: if you come to Athens where I am king,
    I shall, as justice urges me, be your protector. But
    I must tell you now that I will not consent
    to be your escort from this land. If you can find
    your way to reach my house, there will I harbor you,
    and never give you up to anyone. But you must get there
    on your own—for I am a guest here, and wish to keep
    the good opinion of my hosts, and an honored name.   810

MEDEA

    It shall be as you wish. But I would ask for only
    one thing more: your word on this, a promise sworn.

AEGEUS

    Do you not trust me? What makes you doubt the safety I intend?

MEDEA

    I trust you, yes. But I am walled around by enemies—
    the house of Pelias hates me, and Creon too. If an oath
    binds you, then you will not give me up when they arrive
    in force to take me from your land. For what I fear
    is this: that if your words are merely that, and not sworn
    by the gods, diplomacy might win you to comply—
    for I am weak, and they are tyrants: rich and powerful.   820

AEGEUS

    How wise you are, and worldly, too. Well, I have no
    objection to this oath: it will be safer for us both: for me,
    good cause to show your enemies why I refuse them
    your return; for you, a future more certain and secure.
    Speak: I will swear by whatever gods you name.

MEDEA

>Swear by the fruited plains of Gaia, and Helios,
>old sun, my grandfather; and by all the gods that live.

AEGEUS

>What should I swear to do, or not to do? Instruct me.

MEDEA

>That, as long as you live, you will never give me up
>to my enemies, nor banish me yourself from your land.   830

AEGEUS

>I swear by fertile Gaia, by the holy light of Helios,
>and by all the gods, I will do exactly as you've said.

MEDEA

>Good. But say: what punishment for breaking such an oath?

AEGEUS

>The chaos that will always swallow faithless men.

MEDEA

>Go your way, friend, and may joy be your companion!
>For all is well, and I shall come soon to your city's
>welcome haven—when I have done what I must do.
>(*Exit Aegeus.*)

CHORUS LEADER

>May Hermes, Maia's son,
>patron of travelers,
>guide your steps   840
>and bring you
>safely home, and may
>you have your heart's
>fondest wish, Aegeus,
>for you have shown
>yourself most noble
>and generous of men.

MEDEA

Oh Zeus and Zeus' justice, oh light of the ancient sun,
I am exultant, friends; I sense my victory's bright approach:
my foot is on the road. My enemies shall pay in agony   850
their debt to me. For when my hopes were foundering,
Aegeus appeared to set a pharos on a rock, and offered me
safe passage, harbor, all: to Athens I will go, and make
my cable fast to him.
                    Now I shall unfold my whole
design to you: listen, though you will take no pleasure
from my words. I shall send a servant to call Jason
to appear before me. When he arrives, I'll fill him full
of soothing words, say that I now share his views
and see his royal marriage, entered in by leaving me,
a match well made, judicious, advantageous to us all.   860
I shall ask that the children be allowed to stay in Corinth,
though not, be sure, to leave them behind as fair prey
to the insults of my enemies. No, I intend to use them
in a plot to kill the princess. They shall be my messengers
and guile their guide. I shall send them to the bride
to ask her not to banish them, and for a bribe: a gown
as finely woven as a spider's web, a diadem of hand-
wrought gold. If she takes this lovely gift, so irresistible,
and puts it on, why then she dies a painful death,
and so does anyone who touches her—for I will smear   870
these gifts with deadly poisons that melt flesh like tallow
in the fire.
            But here the pleasures of rehearsal end. Woe
is me—I groan to name the deed I must do next.
I shall kill my children: no one and nothing can rescue them.
When the fall of the house of Jason is complete, then I shall
leave the land, flee from the murder of my own dear sons,
the perpetrator of the most unholy deed. But worst of all
is to be laughed at by one's enemies. So I will do this
deed. My life is worthless anyway. I have no fatherland,
no house to call my own, no refuge from misfortune.   880
My one mistake was to leave my father's house, cajoled

by the words of a Greek! But he will pay dearly for what
he's done—a god supports my cause. From this day, never
shall he see his sons alive, nor will he breed more children
on his new bride, wretched woman who will die a wretched
death, and from my venom's power. Let no one think
me weak, the object of their simpering pity or contempt,
but see me as I am—and that the opposite: a scourge
to my enemies, a benefactor to my friends. For those
who act as I do, forever, their names live on in glory.   890

CHORUS LEADER
    You would not have told
    your plan to me
    unless you hoped
    I would dissuade you.
    I would aid you
    in your time of need,
    and yet uphold
    the sacred laws
    of humankind:
    I implore you, Medea,   900
    not to do this deed.

MEDEA
    As if some other act might set it right! But how
    could you understand: you have not suffered as I have.

CHORUS LEADER
    Woman, will you
    really bring
    yourself to kill
    your own offspring?

MEDEA
    By this, and nothing less, I hurt my husband most.

CHORUS LEADER
> And make yourself,
> of all women, 910
> most wretched.

MEDEA
> What must be done, must be. And till it is, all talk
> is but a swarm of syllables in air.
(to Nurse)
> You there,
> my trusted servant, go and bring Jason here. As you are
> true to your mistress, and to all of womankind,
> tell him nothing whatsoever of my plans.
(Exit Nurse.)

CHORUS
> The sons of Erechtheus from the days of old
> were blessed with peace; children of slow ages
> and the gods; no tribe invaded their holy place,
> no horde pillaged it—fortune was theirs, 920
> and sweet repose. Wisdom was their food;
> like birds, their passage brightened the air,
> where once, it is said, the nine Pierian muses
> raised golden-haired Harmonia there.
>
> Aphrodite bent and filled her urn at the streams
> of Cephisus, so the legends go, and made
> the climate temperate, the fragrant breezes
> blow. She hovers in the arbors even now,
> winding roses in her sumptuous hair,
> sends Eros to join Sophia—so joy 930
> enlivens wisdom, blessed pair.
>
> This city of Athens
> whose very rivers flow
> from springs of love,

whose ceremonies bring close
gods and men—how shall
this city harbor you?
You, a killer of your brood,
stained red with infant blood:
shall you lodge among the pure?   940
Think on this slaughter,
we beg you, by your knees,
do not do this awful deed;
Medea, we beseech you—
do not kill your children!

How will you find
the courage of heart
and skill of hand
to undertake this fearful
crime? And when   950
you gaze upon your sons,
will you keep the ice
of your resolve
from melting into tears,
and dry-eyed,
kill them? No.
For when your children
fall as suppliants
at your feet, you
will not wade   960
in their sweet blood.
(Enter Jason.)

JASON
        I have come at your request. For though you hate me,
                        nevertheless
        I will never refuse you a fair hearing. So, woman,
        what more do you require of me, what is it now?

MEDEA

    I beg you, Jason, to forgive my heated words: I rely
on the many acts of love we've shared in all these years
to make you tolerant of me, my thoughtless anger. I do
repent it now, for, on reflection, I reproach myself
this way: "Foolish creature, why am I raving on
against the ones who have arranged things best?   970
Why make myself a thorn in the paw of royal power,
and in my husband's rosy future, who acts in my best
interests by marrying a princess and begetting royal brothers
for our sons? What has come over me? When the gods
have been so kind, should I not put aside my wrath?
Do I not have the children? And aren't we—they and I—
now exiles in need of friends?" I have seen my folly.
How angry I was at nothing! I commend you for your
good sense in contracting this alliance for all our sakes.
I have been a fool; I ought to be sharing in your plans,   980
helping in their execution, standing by the marriage bed,
enjoying my advantage in this new connection with
your bride. Well, we women are—I wouldn't say
exactly bad—but we are what we are. You should not
give like for like, but, as a man of virtue,
forgive our childish nature. I give way to you:
I admit that I was wrong before, over-hasty,
as now I see the greater wisdom of your view.

    Children, children,
come here, come out of the house, come out!   990
(Enter children from the house.)
    Here is your father, greet him with me, join your mother
who puts aside all enmity, makes peace with him
who is so dear to us. We have made a truce; our anger
has dissolved like smoke in air. Take his right hand.
Oh, just now, I think of what is lurking in the future's
dark. My children, will you, as long as you live, stretch out

soft hands just so? Unhappy Medea! For I am
all tears and foreboding when I should be content. As now,
I end the quarrel with your father, my tender feelings rise,
well up, and, without consent, flood my eyes with tears. 1000

CHORUS LEADER

My own eyes fill as well
with pale tears. I pray
misfortune will not stray
further from what can
be borne. I say: enough.

JASON

Woman, I do approve your wise return to sense,
and do not blame you for resenting me before—
anger is the natural response when a woman's husband
takes another bride. But reason has cooled your wrath,
and time restored your better mind, so that you 1010
recognize the true advantage of my plan.
Now you behave as a wise and prudent woman should.
(turning to the children)
Children, my best laid plans have been for you, to make
secure—with the god's help—a future of prosperity and power.
Some day, with your new brothers, first place will be yours
in Corinth. You only need to grow to manhood, and I,
your father, will see to the rest—with the help of whatever
god it is who smiles on me. May I see you come to manhood,
full of health, the envy of your peers, a scourge to my enemies!
(turning back to Medea)
You there, what is this? why do you weep and turn away, 1020
your cheek as pale as your tears? Why do you hear these words
from me, and not feel pleasure in the sound of them?

MEDEA

Really, it is nothing. It was the children I was thinking of.

JASON

The children? But why should you be wretched at the thought
of them?

MEDEA

I gave them birth, and when you prayed that they might live
and grow, pity for them overcame me. Will it be so?

JASON

Have no fear! I will see to that. It shall be so.

MEDEA

I trust your firm resolve, and must fight against my fear.
My woman's nature weakened me, dissolved my strength
in tears.
But formless fear needs action's shaping force;   1030
for that I called you here. The decision is made to exile me
by those who rule this land. I am content with that;
I see that it is best that I not stay as an encumbrance
to yourself, and to the country's king—for I am thought
an enemy of this house. I am resigned therefore to exile
for myself. But, so the children shall know a father's
rule, plead with Creon that they be allowed to stay.

JASON

I doubt he'll be convinced by me, though I will try.

MEDEA

Well, if you think he will be adamant, then tell your wife
to intercede and spare the children exile's doubtful fate.   1040

JASON

Indeed I will, and she, I have no doubt, I can persuade.

MEDEA

Yes, if she is a woman, as the run of women go.
But I shall help you, as needs be—by the children's

hand, I'll send her gifts, gifts far more beautiful
than anything that mortal hands have made. You,
servant, hurry, bring these treasures out to me.
(Exit servant into house.)
How bountifully her happiness will overflow, for in
her bed she has got you—a hero for a husband,
and now she will possess as well these glorious gifts
my grandfather, Helios, god of the sun, gave to his own.   1050
(Enter servant with the gown and diadem.)
Children, take in your hands this bridal dowry, carry it
to the happy royal bride. It is a gift most fitting to her joy.

JASON

Foolish woman, why give up your precious things
to her? Do you think the royal house has need of gowns
or gold? Keep what is yours; don't throw your wealth
away! She is my wife, and so, I feel sure, will value
more my wishes and my word than any wealth of yours.

MEDEA

Say no more. For it is said that gifts win over
even gods, and an ounce of gold is more to mortals
than a wealth of words. Heaven favors her: she is young,   1060
and royal, and has the power we must propitiate.
And, for the children's sake, to keep them always
here—more than mere gold, I would give my life.
(turns to the children)
Children, listen well. When you are in the palace,
entreat your father's new wife, who is my mistress now,
that she speak out against your banishment. And give her
these priceless things—this is most important: be sure
you place them in her hands. Go now, hurry to persuade her.
May these gifts succeed, and may you bring back soon
the good news that your mother longs to hear.   1070

CHORUS
Hope no more, my heart,
no more; the children's
fate is sealed.
They walk the dead-end
road—murder and death
concealed and waiting
there. The bride will
take the bait of gold, and
with her own hands place
the dread tiara on   1080
her lovely hair—
and crown herself
the queen of ruin.

Who could resist the gleaming
fabric of that heavenly
robe, the circlet with its heavy,
woven gold? She will
put them on, gown and
diadem by turn, and so
will make her bridal   1090
with the dead: the snare is
irresistible, the trap
is set to spring.

And you, cursed
husband, who married
into the house of kings—
unlucky, unsuspecting
groom—you bring
destruction to your own:
to your children, doom;   1100
to your bride, a dreadful
end. Unhappy one,

your fate is not to be
the glorious one you sought.
Oh, next, unhappy mother,
loss multiplies your sorrow.
I mourn for you, who mean
to slay your sons, your own
tomorrow—revenge on a husband
who disgraced your marriage   1110
bed, and, flouting law,
put another woman
in your place.
(Enter Tutor with the children.)

TUTOR

My lady, your sons are reprieved from exile. The princess
was delighted with your gifts, and took them from the children's
hands. So the royal power grants them peace.
But why should you be distressed at such good fortune?
Why turn away and show no pleasure at good news?

MEDEA

Alas!

TUTOR

My message and her cry of pain don't match.

MEDEA

Oh gods, alas!

TUTOR

Do I mistake the meaning of my news?   1120
Perhaps I bring report of what I only think bodes well.

MEDEA

You bring the news you bring. I have no quarrel with you.

TUTOR

Then, I am confused. Why such sadness in your eyes?

MEDEA

Old man, my reasons are my own, sufficient for tears.
The gods and I, in my mad rage, contrive despair.

TUTOR

Cheer up: grown up, your children will surely bring you home.

MEDEA

Before that day, there are some I'll send forever home—
wretch that I am. Don't speak to me of home!

TUTOR

You are not the first woman, nor the last, to be divided
from her children. We mortals must bear what fate ordains.   1130

MEDEA

And so I shall. But take your own advice and go
inside, resigned to your own lot in life. My children
are your charge: see they are provided for.
(Exit Tutor into house.)
My children, my children, soon you will have a city and
a home, in which, from now until forever, you will
live, bereft of me. I shall be gone, an exile, to another
land, and shall not have the sweet years to enjoy
your growing up, will never see your happiness, nor
shall I tend your nuptial baths, nor lift your wedding
torches and light you to your marriage beds. I suffer   1140
now, most horribly, from my own implacable will.
Waste, waste . . . it was all waste: those years I brought
you up, the labor and the pain that I endured in childbirth. All waste. I tell you with despair how many
were the dreams that I, hope's fool, once had
for you: I saw you caring tenderly for me in my

old age, and when at last I died, in my posthumous
eye, I saw you bending over me, and dressing me
for burial—the best end that a mortal can enjoy.
But now, as a wind will scatter thistledown, my bright   1150
imaginings grow pale and blow away. And nothing
now shall come of them—they fall on barren stone;
without my sons, my life shall pass in monotone,
one long gray grief. Nor shall you see me more
with your warm, loving eyes, but you shall pass
from me into a place from which I am forbidden.

Oh, children! If only I could read your glance, the look
I take away with me. Why smile this final smile at me?
Alas! What can I do? My courage, women, is all gone
at the sight of the children's bright, trusting faces. No use.   1160
I cannot do what I had planned. Goodbye to my designs.
I shall take the children with me from this land. What use
to wound their father with their pain, and then endure
a pain far greater. No, I will not. Farewell, my plans!

But what has come over me? Should I reprieve my enemies,
and let them go, unharmed for what they did to me?
Must I bear *that*? Should I, Medea, suffer mockery?
No. It is a hateful weakness to let such tender thoughts
erode my settled purpose. Children, go into the house!
Let those who may not lawfully attend my rites of sacrifice,   1170
let them think of the children. My hand shall not falter.

By now the crown is on her head, the robe of fire
around her—the royal bride is dying of my charms.
Of that, I am sure. But—since the road that I must go
yawns now before me: the one that leads me to
the fiercest misery, and them to one worse yet—I want
to say a last farewell. Children, come here to me.

Give me your right hands to kiss, my children. Let me
kiss them one more time. Oh hands and lips most dear

to me, O children, the noble bearing and the open   1180
countenance I love! I wish you happiness—but in that
other place, for the happiness we had here your father
has taken all away. Oh, how sweet is the touch of children,
how soft their skin, how fragrant their lightest breath!
Go in! Go in! I can look at you no more. Pain closes
like a fist around my heart. And I know well this pain
is but a prelude to the one that I shall soon endure,
but rage will bite through reason's curb—how useless to know
that the worst harm comes to us from heedless wrath.

(Exit the children, followed by Medea.)

CHORUS LEADER

    Often before now I have   1190
entered into matters more
subtle, more vexed with
contradictions than are
considered fit for woman's
mind. For we, too, possess
a Muse to touch
our brows with wisdom—oh,
not all of us, by any means,
but there are those among us,
a few to whom   1200
this lucid Muse is friend.
Just now, she bids me
speak of those
who have not given birth,
have not raised children
of their own—those barren
ones are happier than
parents, much to be envied.
The childless, who cannot judge
first hand if children are   1210
a gift or curse to humankind,
are spared much suffering. While

those so sweetly blessed
with children, I see them
worn by never-ending care:
first, they must struggle
to raise their children well
and then to assure them
provision, and a way to get
a living. But, with all of that,   1220
no certainty assures the young
are worth their trouble, nor
does a parent find it easy
to discern the worthy from
the worthless one. Further,
the last of all misfortunes
still awaits. For even
if a child comes of age,
has skills sufficient
to a livelihood, and has   1230
a sterling character—
fate takes a hand, and
here come Death to drag
him off to Hades.
What is the point
that, for the sake of heirs,
the gods have added
to our many mortal cares
this grief that is, of all
our pains, hardest to bear?   1240

MEDEA
My friends, I have for some time been expecting news,
waiting to hear how things have turned out at the palace.
And look, here comes one of Jason's servants now,
his breathing labored, as if disaster clawed his lungs.
(Enter Messenger.)

MESSENGER
Medea, run for your life! Whether by boat on the sea
or overland by chariot, flee by whatever means you can.

MEDEA
But what has happened from which I have such need to flee?

MESSENGER
The princess and her father, Creon, Corinth's king—
murdered! And by your poisons both lie dead.

MEDEA
What splendid news! From this day on, I shall regard you   1250
as a friend, a messenger who brings such welcome news.

MESSENGER
What did you say? Have you gone mad? Woman, can you
outrage justice thus, and in the royal house itself,
and still rejoice? And not show any sign of fear?

MEDEA
As to outrage, there is much that I could say to that.
But calm down, friend, and take your time: tell me how
they died. My pleasure will be much greater if you say
they died, not all at once, but slow . . . in agony.

MESSENGER
All of us, your old servants, who mourned for your
misfortunes, rejoiced when your two children came,   1260
together with their father, into the new bride's house.
The halls buzzed with the happy rumor that all was mended
between you and your husband—your quarrel ended. Someone
kissed the children's hands, another their golden heads.
Myself, out of pure joy, I went with the children
into the women's quarters. The mistress, whom we are
bound to honor now as once we honored you,

had—as usual—eyes for Jason alone. But then she caught
sight of the children, and veiled her eyes as if to blot
them from her view, much displeased that they had   1270
dared to enter there. But your husband sought to soothe
her anger with these words: "You must not," he said, "be
so unkind to those who are now your kin, but turn your
face to us again and love those whom your husband
loves. Receive these precious gifts and ask your father
for my sake to grant these children reprieve from exile."

Her eyes grew large at the sight of the shining garments,
and she agreed to all your husband asked, and hardly
had he and the children gone out the door when she
took the glowing gown and put it on, and set the gold   1280
crown on her head, arranging her hair around it as
she admired her lifeless double in the mirror. Rising
from her dressing table seat, she pranced about the room,
glancing back each time she turned to catch the flash
of slender leg in the swirling of her skirt. But then—
the horror began. Her color changed, her legs buckled
under her, she staggered back and sideways, falling
on the chair, her body shaking like a torn sail in a storm.
An old woman among the servants who must have thought
a god possessed her—a sacred frenzy sent by Pan—   1290
called aloud: "May the god bless you," but even as she did,
she saw the white foam pouring from her lady's mouth,
her eyes starting from their sockets, her skin gone dead
and bloodless white. Then the useless shout was followed
by a wail. One servant ran off to Creon's house, another
to her new husband, to tell them of the bride's affliction.
The house resounded with the sound of footsteps drumming.

In less time than it takes a sprinter to make the hundred-yard
dash, the poor girl came to, looked around her
with the terror of returning consciousness, and groaned   1300
aloud most pitifully. For she was being devoured alive:
the golden crown around her head was now a burning

band of fire, and the fine-spun gown your sons had given her
was eating into her flesh with hungry flames. A living
torch, the wretched woman leapt from her chair, trying
to escape the pain. And twisting her head from side to side,
she tried to throw off the crown of fire, but it was fastened
to her hair, and her frantic tossing only fed the flames.
She fell at last to the floor, a seething mass of flesh,
already barely recognizable. Her eyes ran like   1310
cracked eggs, her lovely face was gone. From the crown
of her head a bloody fire dripped; her flesh slid off her
bones like resin from a torch of pine, as if the poison
had jaws no one could see—though of its work we saw
more than we could bear. And after what we'd seen,
we kept away, afraid to approach or touch the corpse.

But her poor, fond father, who had not witnessed
this calamity, all unprepared, burst into the chamber
and stumbled on the ruined body of his daughter. He
cried aloud, and threw himself on her, and kissing   1320
her, he spoke as if she heard: "Oh unhappy daughter,
which of the gods has done this shameful deed—destroyed you
so cruelly and taken you from me? Oh daughter, let me
die with you!" But when he ended his lament and sought
to raise his aged body from his knees, he was stuck
fast to the dreadful fabric of her dress which clung to him
as ivy clings to the laurel tree, and wrestle how he would,
he could not free himself of her without his own flesh
tearing from the bones. At last, fastened to her death,
he breathed no more, and there they lay: the daughter and   1330
the old father, a sight to wring tears from a stone.
As to what your fate will be—it is not for me
to say. Soon enough your punishment will be
decreed. And now is proved again, what I have known
before: our mortal life is but a shadow. Nor do I
fear to say that those whose eloquence argues
for solace in this insubstantial life, are but
the greatest fools of all. For happiness is forever

out of reach. One may be luckier than another
when it comes to wealth—but no one is happy, ever.   1340
(Exit Messenger.)

CHORUS LEADER
Today fate fastens its talons
on Jason—these disasters he has deserved.

MEDEA
My friends, the hour has come, my eye is fixed on what
I must do now: kill my children with all haste, and fly
from this land. I must not put off what I most fear
to do, for then I give my children up to murder
by a crueler hand. Since they must die in any case,
then let me, who gave them birth, be the bearer
of their death. Heart, put on your armor now! Why
do you quail before the dreadful deed that must be done?   1350
Now, unlucky hand, take up the sword, and with the shield
of my resolve in place, take it and go down the dead end
road to misery that is your fated goal. Be as
the hawk when it impales a mouse—be fierce, do not
dare recall the love you bear your children, nor that
you gave them life. For this one day, forget they are your
own—mourn later, and forever; for even if you kill them,
still, they were dear to you. Oh, how unhappy I am!
(Exit Medea into the house.)

CHORUS
O Earth, O sun whose long rays
pry the lid of darkness up, and light   1360
our way, oh, turn your bright gaze
on this lost woman, who brings
ruin in her wake—hold back
her murderous hand before she soaks
it in her children's blood, before
your race of gold lies in the mud;

her sons, O Helios, are of your seed,
a god's tree must not be pruned
by a mortal hand. O Zeus-engendered
light, prevent this act, bind her   1370
to your will, this Fury,
who, bent on vengeance, tears
her own nest apart.

And oh, unhappy woman, the labor
pains of childbirth are all in vain;
it was for nothing that you bore
these two dear sons, you who crossed
the narrow straits, and slipped between
the clashing rocks—and all for
nought. Why is your rage a torrent   1380
that tears reason from its moorings,
murder after murder, each one
worse than the one before? Abhorrent
to the gods is the stain of kindred
blood. Such killers are pursued
by horrors in the shape of their worst
crimes, their houses cursed.

CHILDREN *(within)*
    Woe is me!

CHORUS
    Do you hear the cry,
    do you hear the children cry?   1390
    Oh, ill-fated woman, mother of misery!

FIRST CHILD *(within)*
    Oh, what can I do? How can I escape my mother's
    hand? Where can I hide? What shall I do?

SECOND CHILD *(within)*
    I don't know. Dear brother, we are lost.

CHORUS

> Shall I go in? Shall *I* go in?
> We should stop the murder of the children.

FIRST CHILD

> Yes! Yes! In the name of the gods, stop her.
> I beg you, help me now . . .

SECOND CHILD

> The trap closes on us . . . oh, the blade . . .

CHORUS

> Woman of stone with a heart   1400
> of iron! You would kill
> with your own hand
> the children that you carried
> in your womb, make yourself
> the evil agent of their fate!
>
> Through all the time that was,
> one woman and only one, has
> taken her own children's lives,
> and that was Ino, maddened
> by the gods when she was driven   1410
> by a jealous Hera from her home.
> And when she saw what she had
> done, with her two sons clasped
> in her arms, she stepped from the cliff
> into the storm-risen sea, joining them
> in death. But now that *this* has happened,
> what horror cannot be imagined,
> what will set the limits of our fault?
> Oh woman, love's slave—
> what sorrows you have brought   1420
> to humankind.

(Enter Jason.)

JASON

> Women, you who stand so near the house, does Medea
> shelter there, she who did such dreadful deeds—or has
> she fled? She will have to hide below the earth itself
> or take wing and find a hiding place in heaven, if she
> thinks to avoid the retribution of a royal house. Does
> she think that she can murder with impunity the ruling
> family, and then escape this house unharmed?
> But leave her to her fate—it is the children for whom
> I am concerned. Those she has so terribly wronged   1430
> will be avenged on her, but I fear for the children,
> that vengeance against her will touch them, too,
> for this ungodly murder was their mother's act.

CHORUS LEADER

> Ill-fated Jason, you can't yet know how deep
> your sorrow goes. You would not speak so if you knew.

JASON

> Knew what? Surely she does not mean to kill me too?

CHORUS LEADER

> Your sons are dead, murdered by their mother's hand.

JASON

> What? What do you mean? Woman, your words destroy me.

CHORUS LEADER

> The truth is what it is. Your children are no more.

JASON

> Where did she kill them: within the house or somewhere else?   1440

CHORUS LEADER

> Throw wide the doors and see the corpses of your sons.

JASON

> Servants, pull back the bar, and let me see both horrors—
> the slaughtered bodies of the boys, and her who struck them
>>   down,
> so I may punish her who shed this blood of mine.
> *(Medea appears above the house in a chariot drawn by dragons. With*
>>   *her are the bodies of her children.)*

MEDEA

> Why shake those doors and try to force the bars, what use
> to search there for the bodies, and me who struck them down?
> Your efforts are in vain. If you have anything to say to me,
> then speak, your words will reach my ears. But with your hand
> you'll never touch me more—this winged chariot, Helios,
> my grandfather, gave to keep me safe from hostile hands.   1450

JASON

> Oh vile creature, despised by the gods, by me, and hateful
> to all of humankind, you could bring yourself to take
> the sword to your own sons, and leave me childless,
> my life destroyed! And having done these things, can you
> still look on earth and at the light of day, knowing
> that this abomination is your act? May you perish!
> I see now what I should have known—that I was mad
> to bring you from that barbarian lair to this bright land
> of Greece. Even then, your hand was cursed—for you
> betrayed your father and the land that nurtured you. Now   1460
> the gods have turned on me the vengeful Fury meant
> for you, a traitor to your kind. For you had butchered your own
> brother before you stepped aboard the fair ship Argo.
> Oh, from the first, your hands were bloody—and when
> you had married me, and, in the pleasures of your bed,
> got children—for that same passion, you murdered them.
> No Greek woman would have dared what you have done—
> yet I wed you instead of them, and so I married ruin.
> For you are not a woman, but a lioness, more savage
> than the sea-monster Scylla, with her six man-eating   1470

heads. But ten thousand insults of mine would not move
you—for you are savage, without shame—just get away
from me, you foul disgrace, your own children's murderer!
My own fate I must bewail, for I shall never
now enjoy my bride, nor speak again to my children
alive, the children I begot, and raised, and now
have lost forever.

MEDEA

                 I could speak at length against your words,
but father Zeus knows what things you have suffered from me,
and what you have brought on yourself. As if you thought
that you could spurn my bed, and make a fool of me—   1480
you and Creon and your little princess laughing while
you wallowed in luxury's fat lap—oh no! Nor was I
going to let old Creon exile me, who gave his daughter
to you, and took my place away. Call me a she-lion or
a monster, as you like, for I have aimed and hit
my mark—my barb forever lodged in your cleft heart.

JASON

Yes, but the grief is yours as well—you share my sorrow.

MEDEA

But what is grief compared to the ridicule of fools?

JASON

Children, what an evil mother dragged you down.

MEDEA

Children, your blood is on your father's hands.   1490

JASON

You know my hands are clean; they did not kill.

MEDEA

No, it was your betrayal of me, your blasted marriage.

JASON

And was a marriage reason enough to slay your sons?

MEDEA

Do you think to a woman a marriage vow is a petty thing?

JASON

If the woman is reasonable, yes. But all your griefs grow huge.

MEDEA

As yours do now, in truth. Then suffer: the children are dead.

JASON

But they live on as spirits to revenge themselves on you.

MEDEA

The gods who keep accounts know well who started this.

JASON

Indeed they know your heart, and they despise it.

MEDEA

Oh, hate me, I care not. But I am tired of your carping voice.   1500

JASON

And I of yours. Our parting is all that I look forward to.

MEDEA

It is my wish as well. How then shall it be done?

JASON

Let me have the children's bodies, to bury and to mourn.

MEDEA

Never. I shall take them to the sanctuary of Hera
on Corinth's hill, and there will bury them myself.
Hera's shrine will keep their graves from being defiled.
And rites I shall ordain, for all the time to come,
to atone for this unholy murder, an annual festival
in this land of Sisyphus. And I shall go to Athens,
to the land of Erechtheus, to the house of Aegeus, son   1510

of Pandion. You shall die a death that fits your life—
a coward's end: struck on the head by the Argo's falling
beam, in full knowledge of the folly of betraying me.

JASON

May the Fury who punishes your children's death, and
bloodthirsty Justice, fall on you and tear you to pieces.

MEDEA

What god or higher power will give ear to you, who
broke his sacred oath, betrayed a stranger in his gates.

JASON

Out with you! Barbarian witch! Child-murderer!

MEDEA

Go to your house! Bury your bride!

JASON

I go—without my sons—I go.   1520

MEDEA

Your suffering is nothing now. Wait till you are old!

JASON

Oh, children, beloved children.

MEDEA

Beloved to their mother, not to you.

JASON

And yet you killed them?

MEDEA

Yes. To break your heart.

JASON

Oh, how I long for them now, my dear, dear
children—how I wish that I could hold them in my arms.

MEDEA

Now you would speak to them, now you would hold
them close, when before you cast them from your side.

JASON

By the gods, I pray you. Let me but touch their tender flesh.   1530

MEDEA

No, I will not. You waste your words on me.

JASON

Zeus, do you hear how I am treated, scorned and driven
off by this foul, child-murdering monster? But
with what force and right I still can claim, I raise
my voice in lamentation, and I call on the gods, on all
those powers that dwell on high eternally, to be my witness
that you have killed my sons and afterward deny me
a father's right to touch their bodies, give them burial.
Oh, that I had never touched you and begotten
them, and had not seen them dead, and by your hand!   1540
*(The dragon-drawn chariot lifts, carrying Medea and her dead
children away.)*

CHORUS LEADER

Zeus on Olympus does
with us what he will,
and what is most unthinkable
to us, is swiftly done.
What we looked for
has not come to pass,
and what we least expected,
came to be. So ends the tale.

Hecuba

Rendered freely into verse by
Marilyn Nelson

Gratitude to the translators who guided this
rendering:
William Arrowsmith, David Kovacs, Janet Lembke,
and Kenneth J. Reckford

It was the beginning of fall semester when David Slavitt invited me
to try to translate the *Hecuba*, a play I knew only from Hamlet's speech, but
knew as a tragedy so deep it moved even a jaded hack actor to tears, making
Hamlet wonder, "What's Hecuba to him or he to Hecuba, / That he should
weep for her?" I would have declined, humble in the face of a great master,
with the excuse that I didn't have time: I was teaching, after all. But I felt
behind Slavitt's invitation an implied double-dog-dare of the kind that
made me as a child walk out, with my arms held wide, on fallen tree trunks
over troubled waters. So I closed my eyes, crossed my fingers behind my
back, and said I'd try a hundred lines or so.

Meanwhile, the semester began. One of my courses was a graduate seminar called "Aframerican Women's Narratives," for which I'd ordered an
extensive collection of slave and freedwomen's narratives and nineteenth-
century black women's spiritual autobiographies, along with an impressive
(I thought) number of critical discussions of the genre. I wound up working
on Euripides' play while reading eye-witness accounts of tragedies that ri-
valed Hecuba's grief. My reading of Euripides was thus guided by compara-
tively contemporary stories of bereavement and betrayal, barbarism, and
unfathomable fate.

Although for the most part I did not tinker with Euripides' lines to make
the parallels more apparent, I have sometimes made his generic descriptions
of slavery more specific. But even his original—glimpses of which I hope I
have seen by overlapping earlier translations, each of them in its own way
fine—presents Hecuba as the distillation of the pain described in the slave

narratives. Her children dead or stolen, her husband slain, her homeland lost forever, her nobility reduced to rags: again and again, I read Hecuba's stories in the slave narratives. Children torn from their arms and sold, lovers beaten and sold or murdered, no place to run, no place to hide, their very bodies a badge of inferiority. Hecuba's story is my great-great-great-grandmother's story, a story every black woman in the New World has learned at her mother's knee. The Aframerican woman's narrative was a door into Euripides' play.

Polymestor was another door. I read somewhere that Troy and Thrace were on Asia Minor, across the sea from Greece. The Trojans and Thracians were considered another civilization, almost another race, by the Greeks. Who, by the way, considered themselves superior. So Polymestor is Hecuba's homeboy, her brother, her ace-boon-coon. On top of that he was one of her husband's closest friends. And as soon as Priam was out of the way and he had his chance, Polymestor had done the unspeakable: betrayed his dead friend's family by murdering their youngest son. And for what? For gold. What a scumbag. I think of Polymestor as a man who would sell his own sister to the slave ships, a Congo king straight out of a Vachel Lindsay nightmare. His greed has made him betray Hecuba and brings him to her now to be executed. Euripides even has him trying to ingratiate himself to the Greeks, fawning and boot-licking. I got a special pleasure out of rendering his comeuppance. I blew the smoke from the barrel of my six-shooter.

Then there are the Greeks, who at this point, since the Trojans are enslaved, are literally the masters. Odysseus is a blow-hard and a hypocrite: a born politician, a phony. Talthybius is only the ennobled heart through which we receive the noble story of Polyxena's dying. But Agamemnon is a full-blown character, a man who does right in spite of himself, a little bit like our Herr Schindler. A weak man with good intentions, a mature man humbled by the surprise of love. A secondary pain of the play, for me, was the knowledge of what awaits him later.

I was struck again and again by the play's feminism. I did not add a whit of it; it's there in every version I've read of the text. Some passages in Hecuba's speeches or the speeches of the Chorus surprised me with their cogency. I wish I'd known this play when I was writing the speech, "Today's Woman," I gave at my high school graduation in 1964.

By mid-semester, my seminar had started to discuss the slave narratives as black feminist theology. Their authors struggle, as Hecuba does, first to comprehend, then, when that proves impossible, to accept the unfathomable injustice dealt them. They, too, struggle to believe that controlling fate is the loving hand of a god (a God). Amazingly, most of the Aframerican women whose stories live on in print made the leap of faith and were converted, by embracing their private understanding of Christ, to self-love and self-empowerment, and finally to freedom. But not before they'd been whipped, seduced or raped, sold or not sold as their mothers or children were sold away from them; not before they'd escaped in danger and darkness, bought their mothers, bought their children, bought themselves. Though *Hecuba* is not an abolitionist play, nor is the slavery practiced by the Greeks the same as that practiced by the Americans, the women in the chorus are facing slavery; their suffering has just begun. The only thing I've really added are a few lines in the last speech of the play, a speech spoken by the chorus. I've alluded to Robert Hayden's great poem, "Middle Passage." I've expanded the choral discussion of "fate" and "necessity" so that readers will understand the complex of thoughts and emotions Euripides' contemporaries would have understood in those words (which, I understand, for them were expressed by one word). And I've added an echo of a Negro spiritual: "Nobody Knows the Trouble I've Seen." It seemed appropriate.

Cast

GHOST OF POLYDORUS, Hecuba's young son
HECUBA, queen of Troy, widow of King Priam
CHORUS of captive Trojan women, now enslaved
POLYXENA, daughter of Hecuba
YOUNG SLAVE WOMAN
ODYSSEUS, king of Ithaca
TALTHYBIUS, Greek messenger
AGAMEMNON, Greek king
POLYMESTOR, king of Thrace
NONSPEAKING
    Polymestor's two sons
    Polymestor's escort
    Slave women
    Slaves
    Greek soldiers

(The shore of the Thracian peninsula, where the Greeks have made camp on their way home from Troy. The ghost of Polydorus appears.)

GHOST OF POLYDORUS
    Back from the depths of death I come,
    back through the guarded gateway
    between Hades
    and the gods and goddesses of Life.
    I come: Polydorus,
    the last prince born to Hecuba and Priam,
    and their last son to die.
    My father, fearing that our great Troy
    might fall to the Greek rabble,
    had me smuggled here to Thrace,   10
    to his old ally, Polymestor,
    king over this fruitful plain

and its horse-mounted people.
With me went a gold fortune;
my father's intention being that,
if Troy should fall,
his surviving children
would not know hunger.

I was the youngest, a boy too small
to bear sword and buckler.   20
And while Troy's proud towers stood
and my brother Hector
bloodied the fields with his spear,
Polymestor took good care of me.
For a while I grew, green and flourishing,
under his sentinel regard.
But Troy fell, and Hector;
the Greeks left our palace a white rubble;
and before the altar built by Apollo's
own holy hands, my father was murdered   30
by Achilles' cut-throat son.

Then my father's good old friend
took off his smile and took up his dagger.
He cast my body into the sea.
For gold he did this; for my father's
golden hopes for us.

My body rides each breath of the surf,
a few inches up, a few inches back,
unprayed for, unburied.

Free of that pitiful flesh,   40
for three days now I have floated
above my mother's pain-bowed head,
since the city fell and she was brought
to Thrace on the way to Greece
as victory's grandest spoil. Now

the becalmed Greek navies restlessly await
an overdue fair wind. For Achilles,
transparent on his tomb, has emptied
their home-bound sails. He claims
my sister, Polyxena, as his rightful prize,   50
the booty his valor deserves.
He demands her beauty, youth
and her royal blood be spilled
in sweet libation on the earth
that covers his bones.

And Fate wills it to happen. Polyxena
will be given to him. Achilles will be honored.
Today Fate leads my sister to her death.
And you, Mother, today will see
two of your last children dead: 60
my sister bloodied in sacrifice,
and my pallid remains in lukewarm surf
washed up at the feet of a slave.
I asked below,
and the gods of darkness are merciful:
They have granted my petition
to be buried by my mother's loving hands.
It shall come to pass.

                    I must go,
for my mother is coming
She has staggered out of Agamemnon's tent,   70
still feeling my ghost came to her
last night in a terror-vivid dream.

O Mother,
enslaved majesty, robbed of everything you owned
except your life, some of the gods must have felt
you owed them this suffering
as payment for years of contentment.
(Ghost of Polydorus exits as Hecuba enters.)

HECUBA

> Lead these weary old bones, children;
> hold this old slave's hands
> as you once held those of the queen.   80
> Give me an arm to lean on.
> Be a crutch for me.
> For my legs are suddenly useless.
>
> O Zeus—light of morning,
> oh impenetrable dark,
> why did the night
> show me such horrors?
> O gods of earth and below,
> defend me from these black-winged dreams!
>
> My little Polydorus. But Polydorus   90
> is safe in Thrace.
> And my dear, sweet Polyxena:
> Take back that infernal vision!
>
> O watchers over earth,
> watch over my son and protect him.
> He is the sole remaining anchor of our house.
> He's safe; I know he's safe
> here in Thrace, in the care
> of his father's good friend.
> Ah, but I dreamed such disasters!   100
> Grief after grief after grief after grief.
> My heart has never before been so shaken.
>
> My prophet son and prophetess daughter,
> Helenus and Cassandra:
> I wish you were with me now.
> You were so skilled
> at interpreting dreams.

I saw a fawn, a little dappled fawn,
torn from my thighs
by a wolf whose fangs dripped blood.   110

And as if that wasn't enough, I saw
Achilles' ghost howling on his tomb,
demanding as his booty
the most beautiful royal woman of Troy.
O gods, take back this portentous dream;
keep my daughter safe!
(Chorus enters.)

CHORUS
Hecuba! Queen Hecuba! We've come
as quickly as we could!

Running from the tents of the soldiers
who won us in the victors' lottery.   120

We are all slaves now, all wretched,
snatched as the Greek kidnappers
painstakingly combed the ruins of Troy.

Even so, I could not lift
the burden you bear.

Lady, we bring more pain.
A new burden of loss.
We overheard, just now,
in full assembly, the Greeks decide
Achilles' demands are just.   130
By majority vote, they have sentenced
your Polyxena to death.
A sacrifice to Achilles' honor.

He has appeared on his tomb.
Achilles, in shining armor.
He raised his hands, and the winds ceased.
In the unearthly silence that followed,
I could hear from the tent
his howling demand
that a great prize   140
was yet owed him.

I heard him, too: "Greeks, brothers,
you sail off
without leaving my grave its prize?"

All the soldiers fell to arguing.
Some said they'd heard it,
and that Polyxena had to die.
Some said they hadn't.

Some grumbled they wanted your daughter,
the fair Polyxena, for themselves.   150

Agamemnon was on your side,
and spoke persuasively
because your daughter Cassandra
now shares his bed.

But Theseus' sons,
both of them important branches
of the Athenian royal tree,
spoke one thought
with twin voices:
They argued that Achilles' grave   160
deserved a sacrifice
worthy of his courage.

They taunted Agamemnon:
"Cassandra's white bed,

or the bloodied spear
of the great Achilles?"

Words flew back and forth.

Until he broke in.
That sweet-talking, forked-tongued,
glad-handing son of Laertes, Odysseus.   170

Until Odysseus harangued the crowd, asking
if one slave woman's little life
counted as much
as the glorious honor of Achilles.

He said he was ashamed to imagine
one of their valorous fallen brothers
complaining in Hades that Greeks
failed to thank the heroes
who died for victory
on the bloodied plains of Troy.   180

And he's on his way here now,
to pull Polyxena from your arms.

Hurry to the temple!
Prostrate yourself before the altar!

Go to Agamemnon;
beg him to let your daughter go.

Beg the gods! Beg heaven,
beg earth!

Only the gods can save you
from being made a childless mother.   190
Pray to them.

Or you will see your daughter,—
hands tied behind her back,—
face-down on the grave,—
blood spreading from her throat—
like a broken necklace of golden beads.

HECUBA
My grief, my grief.
What more can I say?
Can language name my loss?
First to face age,   200
then to descend into bondage:
oh, my grief!
This unbearable pain!
Who can I cry to?
What kin? What home?
My children snatched,
my husband slain,
my city knee-deep in ashes.
Where should I go?
Which of the gods,   210
what mortal power will defend me?
Ah, women of Troy,
evil-bringers,
harbingers of woe,
your words spit death in my face.
Why choose life? How should I live,
whose light has become such darkness?
Feet, poor stumbling old feet,
carry these weary bones
on back to the tent.   220

Polyxena! Daughter, my Polyxena,
come out of the tent!
Your broken-hearted mother

has heart-breaking news for you,
an unthinkable rumor concerning your life.
(Polyxena enters from tent.)

POLYXENA

   Mother, what frightens you so?
   The fear in your voice made my heart rise
   like a flock of starlings.

HECUBA

   Oh, my baby, my baby!

POLYXENA

   Mother, what troubles you so?   230

HECUBA

   My child, I grieve for your life.

POLYXENA

   What is it, Mother?
   You terrify me.
   Feel my hands shake.

HECUBA

   Oh, dear gods, my child!

POLYXENA

   Mother, what are you talking about?

HECUBA

   I've heard a bone-quaking rumor:
   They've decided to take your life.

POLYXENA

   Who has?
   What do you mean?   240

By the gods, Mother,
speak!

HECUBA

The Greeks have decided to spill your blood,
as a sacrifice in his honor, on Achilles' tomb.

POLYXENA

Oh, Mother, not another blow
to your gray head!
Once more the gods rain catastrophe
on their best woman.
A woman already bleak-eyed with despair.

We might have been slaves   250
together, sharing our dreams
like scraps of bread stolen
from the tables we serve.
I might have been comfort to you,
and closed your eyes when you die.

But now I must die,
and right before your eyes,
like a bleeding lamb on the altar.
Held back by strong arms,
you must watch as my breath   260
gutters and goes out,
you must see me sink
to Hades' vast caverns.

I weep for you, Mother,
not for myself.
You will remain a slave.
While I, with my throat slashed,
I shall die, and be free.
(Young slave woman enters, followed by Odysseus.)

YOUNG SLAVE WOMAN
> Look! Here comes Odysseus,
> striding like a messenger   270
> with important news.

ODYSSEUS
> Hecuba, you may have heard
> what the Greeks have decided.
> They voted, almost to a man,
> that your daughter shall die,
> joined with the honor of Achilles,
> the greatest of Greeks.
> They've sent me to be her escort.
> And when she gives her life
> to Achilles' glory,   280
> Achilles' own son will serve as priest.

> You know what you must do:
> Don't embarrass yourself
> by clinging to her,
> nor me, by making me
> tear her away.
> Act like a queen;
> accept your destiny with grace.
> The only rational response
> is to bow before the gods.   290

HECUBA
> O gods,
> when will you tire of tormenting me?
> You've destroyed my home and my family:
> Why don't you let me die?

> Do you keep me alive
> to inflict more grief?

Odysseus, if a slave may be so bold
as to question the free
without giving offense,
may I ask you a question?   300

ODYSSEUS

Go ahead, ask.
I can wait a minute or two.

HECUBA

Do you remember
when you came as a spy to Troy,
in reeking rags, your eyes fouled with blood,
your beard matted with filth?

ODYSSEUS

Of course I remember.
The incident pierced my heart.

HECUBA

But Helen recognized you immediately,
and whispered to me who you were?   310

ODYSSEUS

I knew I was in mortal danger.

HECUBA

You stopped begging for coins,
and instead embraced my knees
and begged for your life.

ODYSSEUS

I even kissed
the dusty hem of your gown.

HECUBA

You were *my* slave then.
Do you remember what you said?

ODYSSEUS

    A man will say anything,
    anything, to live.   320

HECUBA

    And I told you to go?
    I gave you your life?
    I set you free?

ODYSSEUS

    I wouldn't be here
    if not for you.

HECUBA

    Then how can you treat me like this now?
    To take the gift of life from me,
    then thanklessly decree my further misery?
    Yours is the gratitude
    of political ambition: 330
    you betray friendship
    to buy acclaim.

    But tell me: By what reasoning
    was this decision reached?
    What has possessed the Greeks
    to demand a human sacrifice,
    when all the gods require
    is a fine young bull?
    Is it Achilles' twisted vengeance?
    Why does he choose Polyxena?   340
    She never did him any harm.

    If he wants someone to die,
    then let him take Helen.
    He died for her, after all:
    Helen bred his ruin.

If it's beauty he requires,
why, Helen is the most beautiful woman
in the whole known world!
The lovely Helen, whose beautiful hands
opened this Pandora's Box.   350
All I ask is justice, Odysseus,
my just payment
for the life you owe.

You admit you grabbed my hand,
fell to your knees, begged for your life.
Now it is I on aching knees who hold
your hand between my own, and beg,
I beg you, Odysseus: have mercy.
Let her live!
Don't tear my child from my arms!   360
Please don't kill my baby.
Surely there are enough dead already
without her. Surely enough has been taken
from me. She is all I have left:
my only comfort, my only Troy.
You think, because you have power,
good fortune lasts forever.
I know. I was once a queen.
One day made the queen this slave.
My friend, take pity on me.   370
Talk to your Greeks. Make them understand
that what they plan is murder.
Say we are helpless, we are women,
torn from our prayers at the sacred altars.
They spared us then, out of pity.
Plead our case before them. Say their own law
forbids murder; both of the free man
and of the slave. They respect power.
Go to them. If the argument is weak,
it will draw strength from your authority,   380
and resonate with your honor.

CHORUS *(in unison)*
> Surely no one's heart is such a stone
> this shattered-hearted plea
> does not loosen tears.

ODYSSEUS
> Let me set you straight, Hecuba.
> You imagine me your enemy,
> when nothing could be farther
> from the truth. My advice
> was well-intentioned, a kindness
> meant to save your life,   390
> as you once saved mine.
> But Troy is ours, thanks to the greatest
> hero the world shall ever see.
> And he claims his prize.
> Cities, kingdoms, and civilizations
> have fallen for failing to pay
> homage to honor. And Achilles
> was the most honorable
> of all Greeks:
> a great friend, a great man,   400
> and a soldier whose death
> defined the pinnacle of greatness.

> Shall we ignore his just demand?
> What will future generations
> of potential soldiers think
> when they are called to war?
> Will they refuse to fight,
> believing death on the battle-field
> is meaningless, forgotten?
> As far as I'm concerned, life   410
> is sufficient. But when I die,
> let me die with honor,
> a death men will remember.
> For honor lasts forever.

You ask for pity.
But I ask for pity, too. Pity Greek
mothers and fathers, whose children
meant as much to them as yours to you.
Pity the wives and children of Greeks
whose bodies are becoming Trojan dust.   420

Do you think we're wrong to honor
superhuman love and courage in a man?
Would you break faith
with your own heroes?
Perhaps that explains why Fate
blessed us with the victory.

CHORUS
This is what slavery is:
To bear whatever wrong
the master deals. To bear it.
To suffer. To obey.   430

HECUBA
Oh, Polyxena,
my prayers rise in the air,
and blow away.

You must try now.
Beg him. Plead. Sing the nightingale's
high, throbbing requiem, which cannot fail
to touch a heart.

Cling to his knees; look up
with the eyes of his own child.
He may remember him, and have pity.   440

POLYXENA
You fold your arms, Odysseus,
under your woolen cloak,

and turn your face away.
So I cannot, begging, touch you.
Don't worry; I will not beg.
Not you; not even Zeus,
who defends the helpless.

How should I beg
for the life of a slave?
Should I be a coward,   450
and refuse Fate's gift of freedom?

My father was king of Troy.
The very air I breathed
was regal. I was to marry
one of the kings and princes
already jostling each other
to win my attentions.
I was a princess. Everyone bowed
or curtsied when I passed.
I was revered and envied,   460
thought a goddess
in all respects except
that I must die.
And now I am a slave?
The word itself is a death warrant.
Is it life, to stand stripped
on the auction block,
and be sold
to the richest bidder?
Shall I, sister of Hector   470
and other princes,
sweat over the grindstone,
the bread bowl, the scrub brush?
Shall I knead wet sheets
until my back aches,
day after day after day?

Shall a king's bride be forced
in the bed of the slave
who is her master?

No. I choose death.   480
I turn away from the light.
In the darkness, I shall be free.

Here is my hand, Odysseus:
take me away. For I see
there is no hope, nothing to hope for,
and no reason to live.

Mother, please don't try to stop me.
Let me die with dignity,
not live a life of shame.
Shame is new to me: I might learn   490
to bear it, but the weight
of a life without beauty
would surely break me.
I'll die before I'll be a slave.

CHORUS
     "Nobility" is a seal of approval
     stamped on the high-born. But true
     nobility is a mark of greatness.

HECUBA
     Daughter, I am proud of you
     and your noble speech.
     But this nobility tears my heart.   500
     If Achilles must
     have his victim, if this is what Greeks
     mean by honor, then spare her, Odysseus,
     and take me instead.

Take me to Achilles' tomb.
Slaughter me, not her.
For it was my son Paris
whose arrows felled Achilles.

ODYSSEUS

The ghost asked for the girl's blood,
woman, not yours.   510

HECUBA

Then let me die with her:
earth and the ghost will drink
double blood.

ODYSSEUS

One death will do.
One death is enough.

HECUBA

Let me die with her!
I must!

ODYSSEUS

Who's giving the orders here,
the master or the slave?

HECUBA

I'll cling to her   520
like ivy clings to oak.

ODYSSEUS

Listen to me, Hecuba.
For your own sake: don't.

HECUBA

I'll never let her go.

ODYSSEUS

    And I will never leave her here.

POLYXENA

    Listen to me, Mother.
    And you, Odysseus: be gentle
    with the pain of a mother's love.
    She has good reasons for despair.

    Poor Mother,   530
    don't fight higher power.
    Do you want to be thrown in the dust,
    this dear old body bruised,
    strong-armed by some muscle-bound
    Greek teenager?
    You can't do that.
    O Mother, Mama—
                    Give me your hand.
    Press your smooth cheek to mine for one
    last loving kiss.
    And never again.   540
    This is the last time I shall look upon
    the radiant circle of sky.
    These are the last words
    I shall ever speak to you,
    dear Mother, who gave me
    the gift of life.
    O Mother, Mother,
    take back the gift.
    I go below.

HECUBA

    While I slave on   550
    without you, in the light.

POLYXENA

    No bridegroom will undress me,
    no wedding-songs for me.

HECUBA
For you songs of lament, my child.
And for me, shrieking anguish.

POLYXENA
I'll sleep in dark Hades,
an eternity away from you.

HECUBA
Where shall I turn?
O gods, when shall I die?

POLYXENA
Born free, I shall die a slave.   560

HECUBA
I bore fifty children
and I lose them one by one.

POLYXENA
What shall I say to Father and Hector?

HECUBA
Tell them I am the Queen of Sorrows.

POLYXENA
Oh, sweet breast that suckled me.

HECUBA
This is unjust: You're too young to die.

POLYXENA
Give Cassandra my farewell.
Farewell, Mother.

HECUBA
Others may fare well.
Your mother does not.   570

POLYXENA

Farewell, Polydorus,
living safe here in Thrace.

HECUBA

How should Polydorus live,
touched by my luck?

POLYXENA

He lives. When you die,
he will close your eyes
with gentle fingers.

HECUBA

I've already died,
slain by my sorrow.

POLYXENA

Cover my eyes, Odysseus,   580
and lead me away.
I'm not yet dead, but already
my mother's dirge for me
has broken both of our hearts.
Oh light, I can still speak your name,
still catch a glimpse of you
before my eyes grow dim on Achilles' grave!
(Polyxena exits with Odysseus.)

HECUBA

O gods!
I cannot stand!
My legs fail me.   590
Polyxena!
Polyxena, take my hand!
Don't leave me childless!
Gods, I am destroyed.

Oh, to see Helen in her place,
the lovely Helen, whose flashing Spartan eyes
burned Troy's happiness to ash.

CHORUS

O spindrift seabreeze,
you belly sails and drive ships on.
Where are you taking me?   600
Where shall I be chattel?
Shall I be a Dorian slave,
a slave in distant Phthia,
where, they say, the father of rivers
waters wide green meadows?

Shall I serve on an island?
Perhaps on Delos,
where the first palm and laurel
appeared as Leto labored
and bore Zeus twin gods?   610
Shall I learn the songs
the girls of Delos sing
in praise of Artemis, the divine huntress,
and her unerring golden arrows?

Or shall I be taken to Athens,
and put to work embroidering a new robe
for the temple's Athena,
matched champing horses yoked
to her intricately-stitched chariot?
Shall I sew the fall of the Titans,   620
hulking, savage, thrown down
by Zeus' hurled lightning?

And my children.
My mother. My father.
My city, my ruined Troy.

Smoke and ashes, weeping,
lives spilled and spoiled by war.

I shall be a stranger
in a foreign country,
torn from my motherland   630
and taken west as a soldier's slave
in a marriage that is death!
(Talthybius enters.)

TALTHYBIUS
Women of Troy,
where is your former queen?

CHORUS
She is there, Talthybius, at your feet,
weeping into the folds of her robe.

TALTHYBIUS
Great Zeus, do you see us?
Do you care? Or are we dulled
by opiate faith, while chaos rules
indifferently, by a roll of the dice?   640

This was the queen
of world-famous Troy, the wife
of Priam the Magnificent.
Look at her now:
a childless old slave-woman,
a homeless refugee
fallen from the throne
to grovel in the dust.

I am old too,
each day of my future is numbered.   650
But I'd rather die this very instant

than live this wretched woman's fate.
Hecuba, rise.
Please stand up.
Hold your head high.

HECUBA

Go away and let me weep.
Who do you think you are,
to intrude into grief?

TALTHYBIUS

I am Talthybius, my lady,
messenger of the Greeks.   660
I bring word from King Agamemnon.

HECUBA

Have the Greeks decided to let me die?
Tell me that, and you will be
a herald of good news.
All other news is bad.

TALTHYBIUS

I'm sorry. The message I bring
from the sons of Atreus
is as follows: Come
bury your daughter.

HECUBA

I am not to die.   670
They deny me even this.
My poor daughter,
torn from my arms,
joins my other children.
O gods, gods.
But tell me: How did she die?
Was she slain with respect and honor,

or terminated in a cold-eyed execution?
I must know, though the knowledge
flog me senseless.   680

TALTHYBIUS
    I share your pain in the telling,
    for my telling doubles my tears:
    I wept once watching your daughter die,
    and I weep again, telling you.

    The entire army stood at attention
    as Achilles' son led Polyxena through their ranks
    and onto the grave. I stood near the tomb:
    I saw and heard it all. Behind her marched
    the young soldiers picked to be her guard.

    Achilles' son raised a golden chalice   690
    and poured libation to his father's ghost.
    He signaled me to call for quiet.
    "Attention! Attention!" I shouted;
    "Quiet, Achaeans! Silence in the ranks!"
    I heard a gull cry.
    Then he began to pray.

    "O son of Peleus, great Achilles, my father,
    receive this wine as an invitation to return.
    Rise, drink the wine you asked for:
    our gift to you of the girl's blood.   700
    Let us go now.
    Let the winds come.
    Give us homecoming.
    Grant us safe return."

    Thus he prayed, and the army prayed with him.
    Then,
    drawing his golden-hilted sword,
    he nodded to the guards

that they should seize her. But she spoke:
"Wait, Greek pillagers   710
of my city! I give you my death.
I die of my own free will.
Let no man touch me; I offer
my raised throat to the blade.
Free my hands so I can die free
and be freed.
I was a princess;
I shall not die like a slave."

The army roared in approval,
and Agamemnon ordered the ropes cut.   720
In an instant, she ripped her tunic
from white shoulder to bright girdle,
baring gleaming breasts as lovely
as those of an alabaster goddess.
Then she sank to her knees, and spoke
her bravest words:
"Soldiers,
I present my breast to the sword.   ·
Or do you want my throat?
Here: I yield it to you.   730
Do what you must."
And for a moment, torn painfully
between admiration and duty,
Achilles' son hesitated.
Then he raised his sword
and brought it down
on the swan-curve of her throat.

Her blood gushed,
but she somehow managed
to fall modestly, hiding   740
what should be hidden
from lascivious eyes.

The sacrifice fulfilled, some of the soldiers
gathered leaves and strewed them over her,
while others brought pine branches and logs
for her high pyre.
Those who said it was already big enough
were called lazy and disrespectful:
"How can you stand there empty-handed,
bringing no gift   750
for the girl's great courage?"

That ends my telling.
Lady, having told this,
I must add that I think you
of all mothers the most blessed
in her daughter, and the most
cursed by chance fate.

CHORUS

The gods send Troy disasters
like a steady downpour
of scalding rain.   760

HECUBA

Ah, my daughter:
which of this throng of griefs
demands most? I yield to one,
and they clamor around me,
each with its own heart-break. Grief
after grief, a relentless tide of sorrows.
And with this last wave
I find myself drowning
in a sea of mother's tears.
Even so, a cold comfort comes   770
from knowing how free you were
as you died.
Isn't it strange, how thistle ground

cultivated by the gods overflows
the granary, while the good soil the gods forget
grows a dry, uncombed tangle?
Human nature never changes:
the bad stay bad to the end;
the good, even touched by disaster,
are as changeless as stars.   780
Are we born to our nature,
or is it something learned? Surely goodness
is a wise teacher. And a person well taught
comes to understand evil
by seeing the true beauty of the good.
Ah, but these are the aimless arrows
of despair.
(to Talthybius)
Go to the Greeks. Tell them that no one
is to touch my daughter. Have them hold
the crowds at bay.   790
For without tight-ship discipline
armed men quickly kindle to violence.
And the one who is self-restrained
is called a yellow-bellied coward.
(Talthybius exits. Hecuba turns to the young slave woman.)
Bring me a pitcher of sea-water.
I must bathe my child for the last time,
for her burial wedding. For she is
death's loveliest bride.
What mother's keepsake of my own
can I give her? There is nothing left.   800
Nothing precious. Nothing loved.
I'll ask the other slaves
whether something in their tents
has escaped the pilfering eye.
Some doodad someone has smuggled here,
some bright, contraband hope.
(Young slave woman exits.)

Where has greatness gone?
Where has it gone, that airy palace
in which I was happy? My Lord Priam,
we once were blessed   810
with children and other wealth.
I was mother once,
now I am nothing.
All gone, my babies.

And yet
we brag and strut like barnyard roosters:
the rich man so proud and contemptuous,
the politician gobbling great chunks
of the imaginary food of flattery.
We are so vain. Our lives are vain.   820
Happy are they who live between yesterday
and tomorrow. Happy are they
who ask for nothing: their prayers
are the first to be answered.
Happy they whose luck lasts
for one single, blessed, eternal moment.

CHORUS
My fate became doom,
my luck became sorrow, the day
Paris felled a pine on Mount Ida,
and a tree became the mast   830
of the ship he would steer
to Helen's bed—Helen, the loveliest
of all mortals ever gilded by sunlight.

Now grief, and worse than that, destiny
holds me in its unbreakable embrace.
The ripples set in motion by one man's folly
widened to a curse which engulfed all of Troy.
Paris agreed to judge

one goddess out of three
the most beautiful of all immortals.   840
His choosing unleashed
the relentless machinery of war.

Invasion, battle, screams, and my home—
debris through which rats scrabble.
And a Greek girl mourns, too, alone
in her bedroom in Sparta,
or on the bank of the Eurotas, weeps,
remembering; and mothers mourn sons,
tearing their white hair,
clawing their own cheeks bloody   850
in an ecstasy of despair.
(Young slave woman enters.)

YOUNG SLAVE WOMAN
  Sisters, where is the queen?
  Where is Hecuba, the unrivaled champion
  of sorrow? No one else's grief
  can come close to hers.

CHORUS
  Will the untiring pulse of her bad news
  never rest, never sleep?
(Enter two other slaves, carrying a shrouded body on a stretcher.)

YOUNG SLAVE WOMAN
  This is the grief I bring poor Hecuba.
  I can find no soft words
  for what I have to say.   860

CHORUS
  There she is:
  Tell her.

YOUNG SLAVE WOMAN

    Your Majesty, your misery,
    your agony, your torment: It's beyond
    the ability of language to name.
    Is there a word for darkness beyond despair,
    beyond the reach of the faintest glimmer of hope?

HECUBA

    Don't tease me with promised news,
    then hold it back. This isn't news.
    Why have you brought Polyxena here?   870
    Aren't the Greeks already preparing her funeral?

YOUNG SLAVE WOMAN

    She doesn't know.
    She thinks it's Polyxena.

HECUBA

    You mean it's not?
    O gods, not my prophet,
    not my Cassandra!

YOUNG SLAVE WOMAN

    Cassandra lives.
    Mourn for this boy.
(She uncovers the face.)
    Mourn this corpse we found.
    Mourn this shock, this horror.   880

HECUBA

    It's my son! It's my Polydorus!
    It's my Polydorus, safe with our friend
    here in Thrace!
    Let me die! Oh, let me die!
    Oh, my son, my baby,

how, how, how, how?
Now the laments end;
from now on I will shriek
the blood-freezing song of madness!

YOUNG SLAVE WOMAN
Lady, what Furies pursue you?   890

HECUBA
Beyond all believing;
unreal, this shocking news.
Whiplash after whiplash,
I am flogged by grief.
This anguish shall be the one
defining fact of Hecuba's life.

CHORUS
Loss and suffering its meaning.

HECUBA
Oh, my son, my son.
How did you die?
What hand took his life?   900

YOUNG SLAVE WOMAN
I don't know. I found his body,
sodden, on the shore.

HECUBA
Drowned? Or cast into the sea?
Drowned, or murdered?

YOUNG SLAVE WOMAN
The surf washed him in like this.
(She uncovers his torso.)

HECUBA

Oh, no! No!
Now I understand
last night's nightmare.
The dream's black wings
brought a shadow of truth.   910
You were the slain fawn,
in the dream already dead.

CHORUS

Did you dream the murderer's face?

HECUBA

Priam's good friend,
the noble king of Thrace.
Whose lair we thought
a safe refuge.

CHORUS

Your own friend? But why?
Did he murder for gold?

HECUBA

Unspeakable, unbelievable,   920
unimaginable, ungodly,
oh unbearable, this crime!
Is this what friendship means?
You monster!
You child-murderer!
You hacked him up like this?
You killed our son with your sword?

CHORUS

Saddest of all women,
how heavily heaven's wrath
scourges your shoulders.   930

But hush:
Here comes her master, Agamemnon.
Quickly, sisters, away!
(Chorus moves to side of stage. Agamemnon enters.)

AGAMEMNON
Why haven't you come
to bury your daughter, Hecuba?
Talthybius gave us your message,
and none of our men
has laid a hand on her.
For the life of me, I cannot fathom
your bewildering delay.   940
I've come to get you.
The situation is under control;
everything's going beautifully—
If that word can be used
in such a context.

Ho, what's this?
A corpse beside my tent?
A Trojan, too, I judge
by what remains of his tunic.

HECUBA *(aside)*
What shall I do?   950
Should I fall to my knees
and beg for his mercy?
Or should I swallow my pain
and wear the mask of silence?

AGAMEMNON
Why won't you look at me, Hecuba?
What are you saying? And who is this?

HECUBA *(aside)*
> But what if he responds
> by sneering and shoving me aside?
> What if he treats me like a slave?
> Could I bear that further agony?   960

AGAMEMNON
> I'm not a prophet, Hecuba.
> I can't read your mind.

HECUBA *(aside)*
> Could I be wrong about him?
> Am I seeing an enemy
> where I could see a friend?

AGAMEMNON
> All right, Hecuba:
> If you do not wish to speak,
> I do not wish to hear you.

HECUBA *(aside)*
> Without him I cannot fulfill
> my vengeance. Why should I wait?   970
> His help is my only remaining hope;
> I have to take that chance.
> *(She kneels before him, pleading.)*
> I beg you, Agamemnon!
> I implore you, clinging to your knees
> and grasping your conqueror's hand.
> Please, Agamemnon: Help me!

AGAMEMNON
> Do you want me to free you?
> Ask, and it shall be done.

HECUBA

    No, I want revenge.
    Give me that, and I'll stay   980
    your slave for the rest of my life.

AGAMEMNON

    Revenge, Hecuba?
    What do you mean?

HECUBA

    Revenge for something
    you would never dream, my lord.
    You see this body here,
    and my streaming eyes?

AGAMEMNON

    I see them both.
    But how are they related?

HECUBA

    I bore this boy   990
    for nine months in my womb.

AGAMEMNON

    This is your son?
    But how can that be?

HECUBA

    He was not one of those
    who died fighting for Troy.

AGAMEMNON

    You had another son?

HECUBA
Another son died.
The son you see.

AGAMEMNON
But where was he
when Troy was defeated?   1000

HECUBA
His father sent him abroad,
so he would live.

AGAMEMNON
Abroad? Where?
He was the only one spared?

HECUBA
We sent him here to safety.
Here he died.

AGAMEMNON
To Polymestor?
The king of Thrace?

HECUBA
Yes, and with him Priam sent
a casket filled with fateful gold.   1010

AGAMEMNON
But what happened?
Who killed him?

HECUBA
Who but our Thracian friend?

AGAMEMNON
You think he killed him for the gold?

HECUBA
   Yes. As soon as he knew
   Troy had fallen.

AGAMEMNON
   Where was the body found?
   How did it get here?

HECUBA *(pointing to young slave woman)*
   This woman found him on the shore.

AGAMEMNON
   What was she doing?   1020
   Searching for him?

HECUBA
   She went to bring me water
   to bathe Polyxena.

AGAMEMNON
   He must have slashed him first,
   and thrown him dead into the sea.

HECUBA
   Yes, and the sea cast back
   his mangled flesh.

AGAMEMNON
   I'm so sorry, Hecuba.
   Your suffering seems to have no end.

HECUBA
   I'm dead inside.   1030
   I can feel no more.

AGAMEMNON
Has any woman on earth
ever been so cursed?

HECUBA
Only the goddess of despair.
But listen to my reason
for kneeling here in supplication.
And if you think my sufferings just,
I will accept them. But if
you think otherwise, then
give me my just revenge   1040
on that villainous friend
who neither honors the gods above
nor fears those below.
This is a most foul murder.
This man often sat at our table,
toasting us with Priam's best wine.
He was one of our closest friends,
a man we trusted. And this man,
who received nothing from us
but respect and affection,   1050
this man, our friend,
in cold blood slaughtered our son.
Then he did
something even more ungodly:
He left him unburied, unmourned;
cast his body into the sea.

I am a slave, now, powerless.
But the gods have power.
And over them reigns its source,
the law of absolute truth.   1060
The world is balanced on that law:
From it the gods take life;
by it we live and distinguish

right from wrong.
If we fail to punish law-breakers
who murder friends
and dishonor the gods,
then there is no such thing
as human justice.

Have mercy, Agamemnon: 1070
Honor my plea. Help me
avenge this murder.
Like a painter standing back
to see the whole canvas,
look at me and see
wretchedness whole.
A queen once,
I am now a slave;
once blessed with children,
I now have no one   1080
to comfort my old age.
I am now homeless,
more alone than an orphan,
more lost and unhappy
than any forsaken woman
on the gods' flowering earth.
(Agamemnon turns away, wiping his eyes.)
You turn away.
My hope lies gasping.
Oh helplessness!
(aside)
Why do we spend so many years   1090
learning useless skills?
What we most need to know
is the art of persuasion,
for which there are few teachers.
We should all know
how to argue persuasively.

Lacking that wisdom
how can we win?
(to Agamemnon)
    I have seen my children,
one by one, die before me.   1100
I am reduced from queen
to merchandise. And smoke
still rises over Troy.

It may be useless to mention love,
but for love's sake, think
of my daughter. Think of Cassandra,
my beautiful prophet,
who now shares your bed.
Think of nights of delights
you had begun to doubt ever   1110
really existed. Think of her
fragrant hair on your pillow,
her smooth curves curled in sleep
against your thighs. How much thanks
is her tenderness worth?

This dead boy
was Cassandra's youngest brother.
Honor him with vengeance;
honor her by honoring him.

One word more: 1120
If some miracle,
some gift of the gods
could make my whole body
able to speak—talking hands,
talking arms, talking hair and feet—
then I would be a thousand voices
begging in unison
as I clutch your knees.

And all would cry:
Master, brightest light   1130
of all living Greeks,
have mercy. Have mercy
on an old woman.
She is weak; lend your strength
to her vengeance.
Without you, she is nothing.
As a man of honor,
as a just man, side
with honor and justice.
Punish this crime!   1140
(Agamemnon helps Hecuba rise. Chorus move back to center stage.)

CHORUS

    Fate is an incomprehensible conundrum.
    A life: what does it mean?
    By what necessity are enemies
    destined to be friends,
    and allies mortal enemies?

AGAMEMNON

    My poor Hecuba.
    I feel your loss.
    My heart goes out to your request.
    For the sake of justice and the gods
    I'd like to find a way to help you.   1150
    But no word must escape.
    No one must know that I conspired,
    for the love of Cassandra,
    to assassinate the king of Thrace.
    Polymestor, you know, is our ally;
    your son the son of the enemy king.
    You love him, but the Greek army does not.
    Look at it through my eyes, Hecuba:
    I'd like to help you.

But only if I'm sure   1160
our army won't find out.

HECUBA

So no one living on earth
is truly free.
We are the slaves
of money, the slaves of destiny,
slaves of what people will think,
slaves of obedience to unjust laws.
Slavery makes us act against conscience,
bowed under the yoke of majority-rule.
Master,   1170
let a slave
set you free from fear.
Stand with me
as I do what the heart knows is right.
Be my secret accomplice:
If the Greeks try to interrupt
the Thracian's feast on his just deserts,
hold them off without revealing
that you act on my behalf.
Don't worry: I'll handle the rest.   1180

AGAMEMNON

How?
Are you thinking of poison?
Will you wield a broadsword
with your gnarled old hand?
You'll need strong arms to help you.
Is there someone you can trust?

HECUBA

Your camp is full of Trojans.

AGAMEMNON

You mean our prizes? The women?

HECUBA

    They will help me win vengeance.

AGAMEMNON

    What, women? Are you saying   1190
    women will overcome men?

HECUBA

    If we outnumber them,
    and use our intuitive wiles.

AGAMEMNON

    But women will make war?

HECUBA

    Why not?
    Didn't women kill Aegyptus' sons?
    Didn't Lemnos' women rid
    their city of men?
    Is this enough such proof?
    Give this woman your safe conduct   1200
    through the Grecian camp.
(to young slave woman)
    Go to the King of Thrace. Tell him:
    "Hecuba, once Queen of Troy, bids you
    come to her on a matter which concerns
    your best interest. Bring your sons.
    The matter concerns them, too.
*(Agamemnon signals to two soldiers to accompany the woman. They
          enter, shrugging to each other, then stand on either
          side of her. The three exit together.)*
(to Agamemnon)
    And you, Agamemnon,
    delay my daughter's funeral
    until brother and sister—
    my doubled griefs—   1210
    can burn in a single flame.

AGAMEMNON
>   As you wish.
>   If we could set sail now,
>   I would not agree to this.
>   But the ships still lie at anchor,
>   their sails slack.
>
>   It's for the good
>   in every man and nation
>   that the evil be punished
>   and honors heaped on the good.   1220

(Agamemnon exits.)

CHORUS
>   Oh Troy, my ravished motherland,
>   your name will be forgotten
>   by cities which yet live.
>   A cloud of Greeks descended,
>   and rose again over your ruins.
>   Your crowning towers shorn,
>   you lie stained by flames.
>   Oh my city, my lost Troy,
>   I shall never again
>   set foot in your streets.   1230
>
>   My fate came at midnight.
>   The day's chores were done,
>   and the songs, the dancing,
>   the evening's offering to the gods.
>   I could hardly keep my eyes open.
>   My husband already slept,
>   his spear in its place on the wall,
>   while a thousand silent soldiers
>   neared our shore with muffled oars.
>
>   I had braided my hair   1240
>   and was tying the ribbon in a bow,

sleepily gazing into my gold mirror's
endlessly multiplying light. I was just
ready to go to bed, when shouts and screams
shattered the stillness,
and I heard men cry:
"Forward, you sons of Greece!
For your fatherland!
Destroy Troy so we can go home!"

I was wearing only a short tunic,   1250
like those little girls wear in Sparta.
I cried aloud to Artemis beside our bed,
but I received no miracle.
They slew my husband as I watched,
and I found myself bound
on the deck of a ship, as Troy
slid toward the horizon.
My mind was numb with grief.

Curses on Helen,
sister of the twin sons of Zeus!   1260
Curses on Paris,
whose overweening judgment
brought disaster to Troy!
Curses on their adulterous marriage,
which destroyed my marriage and made me a slave!
May the winds never blow Helen
back toward Sparta! May the sea
never take her home to Greece!
(Polymestor and his sons are escorted in.)

POLYMESTOR
My dear Hecuba,
wife of my poor friend, Priam.   1270
My heart goes out to your loss.
I mourn with you for your city,
and for your daughter's recent death.

Ah, what certainty
can we count on?
Life becomes death,
greatness topples,
good plans go awry.
Nothing endures;
everything vanishes.   1280
The gods create chaos,
rocking the boat until,
half swamped, we believe
and cry to them for help.
But why complain to them?
You are left with your sorrow.

My dear Hecuba,
you must have wondered why
I didn't come to you sooner.
I hope you aren't angry.   1290
I'm sorry: I was away
in the highlands of Thrace
when I heard of your arrival.
I had just
come back home, and was
just on my way to see you
when your messenger, breathless,
presented your summons.
I've come as quickly as I could.

HECUBA

I'm ashamed to let you see me   1300
in this fallen state, Polymestor.
You knew me as proud,
a happy queen. How can I raise
my eyes to yours?
Don't think me rude:
Trojan custom forbids a woman
to gaze directly at a man.

POLYMESTOR
> Yes, certainly.
> You sent for me
> about a matter of urgent   1310
> business, I understand?

HECUBA
> Yes. A personal matter
> concerning you and your sons.
> May we speak privately?

POLYMESTOR *(gesturing to his escort)*
> Wait. There. I'm in
> no danger here.
(Polymestor's escort leaves.)
> Now we can speak freely.
> What is this urgent private business?
> My dear Hecuba, how may I help you?
> Let one of the lucky few   1320
> offer his service
> to a friend less fortunate.

HECUBA
> But first, how is Polydorus,
> in the sanctuary of your home?
> Does he, at least, live?
> My business will wait.

POLYMESTOR
> Of course he lives.
> In him you have good luck.

HECUBA
> My dear friend,
> how like you   1330
> to be so kind!

POLYMESTOR
>What else
>would you like me to tell you?

HECUBA
>Does he miss his mother?

POLYMESTOR
>Yes. One day he tried
>to sneak out and run away
>to see you.

HECUBA
>And Troy's gold is safe?

POLYMESTOR
>Yes, safe in my treasury,
>under watchful guard.   1340

HECUBA
>Keep good watch, my friend.
>For wealth is a great temptation.

POLYMESTOR
>There's no chance of my being tempted:
>I already own all the wealth I want.

HECUBA
>Have you guessed my business
>with you and your sons?

POLYMESTOR
>No. Do tell me what it is.

HECUBA
>My business concerns you,
>my friend. My friend,

for whom my deep and abiding love   1350
is no whit less
than that you have shown to me.
My dear old friend . . .

POLYMESTOR

Yes, yes. What is this business?

HECUBA

Troy's buried treasure,
the ancient riches
of Priam's house . . .

POLYMESTOR

You want me to tell your son
where the treasure is hidden?

HECUBA

Exactly. I know you   1360
will not betray my trust.

POLYMESTOR

But why did you want
my sons to come?

HECUBA

Your sons should know, too,
in case something
should happen to you.

POLYMESTOR

Ah, yes. A wise precaution.

HECUBA

Do you know where Athena's temple
until recently stood in Troy?

POLYMESTOR

    The treasure's there?   1370
    How is its hiding-place marked?

HECUBA

    A black rock juts up from the ground.

POLYMESTOR

    Is that all? Do you have more to say?

HECUBA

    There are also my jewels.
    I smuggled our best heirlooms
    out of Troy. May I give them
    to you for safekeeping?

POLYMESTOR

    Do you have them on your person?
    You've hidden them?
    Where?   1380

HECUBA

    In a tent,
    beneath Greek plunder.

POLYMESTOR

    A tent? In a Greek tent?
    In a tent full of soldiers?

HECUBA

    We captives are assigned
    to women's quarters.

POLYMESTOR

    Can I trust the tent to be safe?
    Is it free of men?

HECUBA

    No men, no soldiers:

    only us women, alone.   1390

    Quick: come inside.

    The Greeks are eager

    to sail for home.

    Our business quickly concluded,

    you may take your sons

    to the place where my son waits.

(Hecuba shows Polymestor and his sons into the tent.)

CHORUS

    The price of life is death.

    Now you must pay.

    Like a man overboard

    you will struggle with terror   1400

    and sinking dread,

    your life pouring past your eyes.

    The life you stole doubled your debt.

    Now you owe both justice and the gods.

    The road you chose to happiness

    from here on careens downhill

    to end at Hades' iron gate.

    And hands unused to weapons

    shall speed you there.

(Brief screams of children.)

POLYMESTOR *(within tent)*

    My eyes! My eyes!   1410

    Oh, I am blinded!

    I cannot see!

CHORUS

    That scream, that anguish!

    Do you hear?

POLYMESTOR
    My sons! Help! Murder!

CHORUS
    In the tent, new horror.
    (Furious scrabbling on tent wall.)

POLYMESTOR *(within)*
    Run, will you?
    Damn you, I'll catch you
    if I have to rip these walls apart!

CHORUS *(individually)*
    Look! He pummels the walls!   1420
    Should we do something?
    Yes! Hurry!
    Hecuba needs us!
    (Hecuba emerges from the tent.)

HECUBA
    Go ahead, pound your heart out!
    Scrape! Scrabble! Tear
    at the walls with your teeth!
    Nothing you do can make your eyes
    see light again, or see your sons alive,
    whom I have killed!

CHORUS
    You did it? You've done   1430
    what you just said?

HECUBA
    Wait, and see for yourselves.
    He'll come staggering out,
    finding his way with outstretched hands.
    You'll see the bodies of his sons,
    slain by my friends and me.

His debt is paid in full.
Shhh. He comes,
in a blind charge.
I'll stand here, away   1440
from his unstoppable rage.
(Polymestor enters, groping about for the women.)

POLYMESTOR
Where? Where?
Where are they?
Where shall I run?
Where shall I stop?

They've made me a beast,
on four feet following
a faint, zigzagging track.
Are you here?
(gestures)
Here?   1450
(gestures)
Where are the hags hiding?
Where are the murderesses?
Where are the harridan,
fiendish daughters of Troy?
O Holy Sun, have mercy
on these blood-streaming eyes!
Give back my light!

Shhh. Footsteps,
small, light: Women. Prey.
In what direction should I leap   1460
to gorge myself on living meat,
to drink my fill of steaming blood?

But no. What am I thinking?
Shall I leave my children

to be torn by the harpies,
to be tossed out, to be devoured
by a pack of mangy mongrels?

Where? Where?
Which way shall I run?
Like a wind-abandoned ship,   1470
I stand helpless, with limp sails.
Where shall I go to guard my sons
from the Trojan hags?
Where is the women's lair?

(Women carry the dead children from the tent. Polymestor, accidentally
bumping into one of them, recognizes the body by
feel. He follows, clinging to the dead. The women
put them down on the spot where Polydorus'
body lay.)

CHORUS

Unhappy man,
you bear unbearable torment.
By the gods, you suffer now,
paying for your crimes.

POLYMESTOR

Guard! Thracians! Help!
Bring your spears to my aid!   1480
Greeks! Sons of Atreus!
Help! Wrong has been done
to the king of Thrace!
I am destroyed by women!
My sons are murdered!
Help me! Help!
Where? Where?
Where shall I take this ruined life?
Shall I fly to black-raftered night,

where Orion hunts   1490
with his dog at his heel,
star-bodies flaring light?
Or plunge to the black river
and onto Charon's silent ferry?

CHORUS
We cannot blame this man
for wanting to die.
Any man would break
under the weight of his anguish.
(Agamemnon enters, escorted by Greek soldiers.)

AGAMEMNON
What is the meaning of this uproar?
Its echo, ricocheting off the cliffs,   1500
has disturbed my soldiers' peace.
If we didn't know Troy had fallen
before our spears, these shouts and screams
might have caused real panic.

POLYMESTOR
Agamemnon!
I recognize your voice!
My friend, good Agamemnon,
see what they have done to me.

AGAMEMNON
By all the gods, what an awful sight!
Polymestor, who blinded you   1510
with these tears of blood?
Who slew your boys?
What a savage grudge
he must have harbored
against you and your sons!

POLYMESTOR

>Hecuba did it.
>Hecuba and those other
>Trojan she-devils.
>They have destroyed me.
>No. They have more   1520
>than destroyed me.

AGAMEMNON

>Did you do this, Hecuba?
>I am shocked, shocked . . .
>Can this atrocity be the work
>of your motherly hands?

POLYMESTOR

>Hecuba? She's here?
>Turn me toward her,
>lead me to her,
>and I'll tear her
>into a thousand pieces!   1530

AGAMEMNON

>What are you doing?

POLYMESTOR

>By the gods, let me at her!
>I'll rip her open
>from chest to cleft!

AGAMEMNON

>Stop! Enough of this barbarism!
>I shall hear each of you speak
>and judge fairly between you.

POLYMESTOR

>Here's the whole truth, Agamemnon.
>Hecuba's youngest son was Polydorus.

Priam, his father, fearing Troy would fall,   1540
sent the boy to me to raise.
I killed him: I admit that.
But killed him for good reason,
and for your sake.
I knew that if the boy lived,
he would someday resurrect
your scattered and broken enemy.
And that you Greeks,
knowing he lived,
would raise another army   1550
and again make war on Troy.
In either case, passing-through soldiers
would trample Thracian wheat
and roast our cattle in the fields.
In either case, Thrace would again
taste Trojan defeat. Thrace
has suffered in this war, too.
Agamemnon, I killed for peace.

But Hecuba heard of her son's death,
and lured me here with a promise   1560
to reveal the secret of Priam's buried gold.
She tricked me into taking my sons,
unguarded, into a tent
with her and a few of her women.

They led me to a couch,
fluffed pillows, seated me,
and bade me welcome.
Sitting beside me and at my feet,
some of the women ran their fingers
up and down the cloth of my robe,   1570
praising Thracian weavers.
They stripped it from me
and took it to the door,

to see it in better light.
Other women oohed over my spear
and slipped it from my hands.

Meanwhile, those women who said
they had children left behind in Troy
cooed over my sons,
smoothed their hair   1580
and pinched their dimples,
passing them from hug to hug
until they were out of my reach.

Then, right in the middle
of seemingly perfect hospitality,
they drew daggers from their robes.
Some of them butchered my sons,
some pulled me down,
held my arms and legs.
I lay helpless, pinned   1590
by the soft weight of women.

And then they did their worst.
They took off their brooches
and stabbed my eyes.
They stabbed my eyes!
They took their brooches
and stabbed my eyes!
Then they ran away,
but I could hear
them panting.   1600

I staggered up,
groping and stumbling
on my hands and feet,
and stalked them, howling,
like a wounded lion
stalks a pack of jackals.

This is my reward
for trying to help you,
Agamemnon. This is my thanks
for killing your enemy.   1610
Your peace cost my pain.

One more thing.
Women: If men have despised them
in the past, do now, and will forever
despise them,
I offer this
experienced truth:
There is no monster
more loathsome
on earth or in the sea   1620
than woman.
Let men beware.

CHORUS

Don't curse women
for evils you have heaped
on your own head.
We are not woman,
we are women:
each unique in her worth
and individual in her entrapment.

HECUBA

Agamemnon, actions speak louder   1630
than words. Good lives
speak truth; evil acts
are lies which rot on the tongue
and spew from unclean lips.
How cleverly the evil
transform good to bad
with a whitewash of argument,
pulling good people

into the spider's web.
But they, too, must   1640
die in the end,
and each plead his case
to the implacable ear
of true, inescapable
justice.

These were
my opening remarks.
Now to my rebuttal.

This man alleges
that he killed my Polydorus   1650
for you, Agamemnon,
to protect Greece
by averting a future war.
(to Polymestor)
      But isn't it true
      that Greece has never
      extended friendship
      to Thrace? Greece frowns on
      alliance with barbarians.
      So why would you murder for Greece?
      Did you think to win   1660
      a Greek wife?
      Did you think to become
      Greece's brother by marriage?

This is a spurious motive.
Did you kill
to protect Thracian wheat
from an army's trampling feet?
Do you think we are stupid?
Who could believe that lie?

But you had a motive true   1670
beyond the need of proof;
a motive which I shall, however,
prove beyond doubt.
You are a greedy, evil man, Polymestor.
You killed my son for gold.

No? Let us consider the evidence.
Why, when Troy's walls still stood
and Priam ruled a great army
led by Hector's all-vanquishing spear,
why didn't you then, if you wished   1680
to make nice to the Greeks,
why didn't you kill my son then,
or offer him to Greece
as a prisoner of war?
But no—
You waited until Troy's lantern
was extinguished, and smoke rose
over her ravaged ruins.
Only after Troy fell
did you murder the innocent guest   1690
who called your hearth home.

And furthermore, why,
if you wanted so much
to ingratiate yourself with Greece,
didn't you give Greece the gold
you admit you held in trust
for its defeated enemy?
Didn't that gold
rightfully belong to Greece?
Surely you knew Greece   1700
would have welcomed
a generous contribution

to its war-depleted treasury.
But the gold lies in your vault,
even as we speak.
Moreover, if you had fulfilled
your sworn pledge
to raise our son to manhood,
men would call your word good,
and honor your name   1710
as a friend in need.
For need proves friendship,
separating real
from convenient friends.
And if someday you were in need,
your foster son, if you had let him live,
would have sped to your side.
In killing him
you killed a friend.
So your gold is lost,   1720
your sons are lost,
and you wander in the dark.
(to Agamemnon)
Agamemnon,
if you acquit this man,
you become his accomplice.

This man betrayed his trust,
broke faith with his guest,
and transgressed the laws of heaven
and of earth.

If you find him innocent,   1730
you are as guilty as he.
If a slave may be excused
for speaking so boldly
to her master.

CHORUS
> Bravo, Hecuba!
> How brilliant your argument
> for the cause of justice!

AGAMEMNON
> I've always had misgivings
> about sitting in judgment
> over other people's woes,   1740
> but I see I must. To accept
> and then shirk responsibility
> is to live in the shadow
> of shame.

> Therefore, here is my opinion.
> The evidence makes the facts clear:
> Polymestor, you killed the boy
> who was at home under your roof,
> neither for me nor for the Greek cause.
> You killed him for his gold.   1750
> We Greeks call that murder.
> And I find you guilty as charged.
> How could I hold my head high
> if I found otherwise?
> I couldn't. Never.
> You committed the crime;
> now accept the punishment.

POLYMESTOR
> You find against me?
> Oh gods, I am bested
> by a woman! Beaten   1760
> by a slave!

HECUBA
> Your crimes have brought you
> face to face with justice.

POLYMESTOR
>   Oh my grief!
>   My sons! My eyes!

HECUBA
>   Why, does your grief hurt?
>   Poor man. Did you suppose
>   my grief did not?

POLYMESTOR
>   Does mocking me
>   make you feel better?   1770

HECUBA
>   Better? What is better?
>   I have my revenge.

POLYMESTOR
>   Enjoy it while you can.
>   For I predict you will . . .

HECUBA
>   Be taken
>   across the sea to Greece?

POLYMESTOR
>   You will drown
>   before the ships see harbor.

HECUBA
>   Pushed overboard, I presume.

POLYMESTOR
>   You will fall   1780
>   from the tip of the mast.

HECUBA

    From the mast?

    And how shall I get up there?

    Shall I fly?

POLYMESTOR

    Climbing, you shall become

    a dog. A bitch with eyes of fire.

HECUBA

    Ah, a dog.

    A mast-climbing dog.

    And, pray, how do you come to know

    of my amazing metamorphosis?   1790

POLYMESTOR

    The prophet Dionysus

    saw it clearly.

HECUBA

    Didn't he also foresee

    your fate?

POLYMESTOR

    If he had,

    you would never have trapped me.

HECUBA

    I shall die, then?

POLYMESTOR

    Die.

    Sailors will call your tomb . . .

HECUBA
No doubt   1800
something having to do
with my transformation.

POLYMESTOR
"Cynossema: Bitch's Rock,"
a landmark on the waters.

HECUBA
What difference
does death make?
I have won justice.

POLYMESTOR
And Cassandra,
your one remaining child,
must also die.   1810

HECUBA
Oh, what hate-filled words.
I spit your prophecies
back at you: May they
foretell your further ruin!

POLYMESTOR
She shall be killed
by this man's
(points to Agamemnon)
bitter wife
who waits for him at home.

HECUBA
Clytemnestra?
Impossible.   1820

POLYMESTOR
   She will kill him, too.
   With the same bloody ax.

AGAMEMNON
   Are you mad?
(He shakes Polymestor.)
   Are you trying to make
   more trouble?

POLYMESTOR
   Go ahead: Kill me.
   That won't keep you
   from the bloodbath
   of homecoming.

AGAMEMNON *(gesturing to soldiers)*
   Take him away!   1830
   Get him out of my sight!
(Soldiers seize Polymestor.)

POLYMESTOR *(to Agamemnon)*
   Does your grief hurt now?

AGAMEMNON
   Shut him up!
   Gag him!

POLYMESTOR
   I have said everything
   I had to say.

AGAMEMNON *(gesturing)*
   Take him away!
   Take him away!
(Soldiers start to remove Polymestor.)

Throw him on some
deserted island   1840
where no one will hear
his wretched lies!
(Soldiers and Polymestor exit.)
Hecuba, go now
and bury your two children.

The rest of you, go
to your masters' tents.
We will break camp.
For the wind we prayed for
has suddenly risen.
May this fair breeze bring us home.   1850
May our long ordeal be done.
(Exit Agamemnon with soldiers. Hecuba slowly enters the tent.)

CHORUS
We must go
to our masters' tents.
Nobody knows why
what will happen to us
there must happen.
From the harbor
we must voyage
to life upon the shore
of bondage. Nobody   1860
knows why this must be.
Fate knows no mercy.
Necessity is hard.
Why must everything
happen as it must?
What is this "must,"
and why? Nobody knows.
Nobody knows.

Andromache

Translated by
Donald Junkins

Translator's Preface

For Kaimei

I committed myself to the task of translating *Andromache* in 1974, and made sixteen "finished" versions in the following twenty-two years. Some speeches, especially Andromache's opening fifty-five-line elegy, went through more than thirty versions. As each failed version narrowed down the list of available experiments, or liberties with Euripides' text, I got glimpses of what it was exactly that I was listening for in my ear and looking for in my lines. I was heady with William Arrowsmith's idea of translation as loyal improvisation,[1] but my improvisations ranged wide and far in my neglect of metrics at the expense of ideas, and in my free wheeling rhetoric at the expense of tone. Over the years, however, as I accepted more formal pressures on my own language, I began to get access to what I at least felt to be the subtleties of Euripides' language. Whatever presumptions that are fueling that idea, it allowed me to keep resuming my quest for a version that I believed would be available to me if I kept working.

I mean by formal pressures the various problems that poets pose for themselves that accompany the solving of the problem of content. In the solvings, or creations, that arise from the original need to invent with language reside the stuff, for want of a better word, of tone. Tone tells all. Content is merely the end result of the poet's discoveries of his or her tone in pursuit of an idea. Because formal structures underlie the formalities of lines and stanzas, design itself can only be discovered, or achieved, depending on one's view of the creative process, if patterns or forms of expression are woven into the discovering fabric of the lines.

All this is to say that in the twenty-plus years I worked on and off on the

1. Arrowsmith, "The Lively Conventions of Translation" in *The Craft and Content of Translation*, ed. Arrowsmith and Roger Shattuck (New York: Doubleday Anchor, 1964), p. 188.

translation of *Andromache*, I began to see the richer possibilities in more formal schemata than I originally realized. At first my ear was listening for lines and phrases that would be dramatic, actable, visually graphic, differentiating each character from another in a stage environment ripened with the invisible presences of gods and goddesses and imbued with the concepts of power and destiny. This was not a bad goal, but it was without the studied interplay of metrics that forced refusals and allowed discoveries of tone revealing content: such mundane things as end rhymes, internal rhymes, equivalent speech and choral lyricisms.

Interestingly, for me if for no one else, I began and ended with the same image in my mind's eye and ear for the character of Andromache. Even though I failed for years to define her satisfactorily in my versions, I always thought of her in terms of Irene Pappas, whom I had seen do a version of *Iphigenia in Aulis* in the early 1960s and in the movie *Zorba the Greek*. I also thought of her as hooded, much like the statue by Augustus St. Gaudens created for Henry Adams as a memorial to his wife Marian, in the Rock Creek cemetery in Washington, D.C. I had remembered Irene Pappas as dignified and expressive, stagewise, self-contained. The statue was the fullest feminine presence I had ever seen; it was grief internalized, serene. Even before I myself had even partially internalized the character of Andromache in Euripides' play, I sensed her presence as like these two figures. I also knew that I had to create this feeling in Andromache's opening speech. And for that opening speech the first several lines were the most difficult for me. They were the last lines to fall into place, twenty-one years after my first attempt. This is how I started:

ANDROMACHE
Asia is gone.—and Thebe has disappeared with it,
the city that brightened my childhood,
the face of my home,
my lovely Asia, gone.
O Thebe, I left you in the sun, riding—
I rode on a golden gleam to far-off Troy,
to the emperor's palace, shining
at the head of a gold caravan, winding
to Priam with my father's gifts. Thebe, . . .

This opening speech went on for 111 lines, double the Greek. The key word, "*skerma*," got pushed down into the second line. It is the word for "metaphor" in Greek, but also means ornament, source of pride, characteristic state, outward appearance, beauty, comeliness, decoration, reputation; it is a woman's image that gives her characteristic imprint, her selection of jewels or dress. Over the years, I tried such versions of the opening lines as:

> O Thebe, my home . . . Thebe, my city, the brightest face
> in all Asia, how far away you seem
> shining in the sun—
>   the day I left
> I, too, was shining, shining in gold, my dowry was pure gold
> and I glittered through all the streets of Troy
> to the great King Priam's palace: Andromache . . .

and this:

> Oh Thebe my city, countenance of Asia,
> I was a girl when I left home for Hector's bed.
> They gave me away. They showered me in gold
> and I glittered in the sun.
>   I was supposed to make sons
> in one of Priam's royal bedrooms. So I did . . .

and this:

> O Thebe my home city, countenance
>   of the whole Asian earth,
> long ago I left you, glittering in my wedding
> gold for the hearth of King Priam, a gift
> for Hector's bed, to make sons in dignity.
> Those were the Andromache years—I was envied then.
>   Now I'm a fated woman . . .

Each of these versions demonstrates in obvious or subtle ways the attempt to accommodate both the literal and whatever the translator chooses to mean by Arrowsmith's "loyal improvisation." In his *Bakkai*, Arrowsmith himself chose to make one of his characters speak in American Southern dialect. Some critics feel that this is quite effective. Examples of improvisation by other translators are legion. In my own original version of Andromache's opening speech I had her report Hector's death under Achilles' ax because I thought it would be good to make a rhyme with Andromache's son Astyanax, who was thrown off the towers of Troy. It probably makes little difference how Hector died in history or in the myth, but since there is no ax in the *Iliad* or in Euripides' version I ultimately took it out. It's still not a bad rhyme. What makes the determining difference, ultimately, is the overall tone of the speech, not the significant details, although, obviously, sometimes the more graphic the details the better. The question is just how expensive and how significant. When I say that tone determines the difference, it's like saying that all wars are local. The exaggeration of detail lends itself in some accumulative way to a slight exaggeration of character. I'm glad I waited the twenty-one years for what I finally settled for. My final version of Andromache's opening speech, created only in 1995, reads:

> O Thebe, Thebe! You were the shining face of Asia
> when I rode away on that caravan, a little golden girl
> riding her father's treasures to Troy, dowry
> for Priam, daughter for the palace hearth, for Hector to
>   make sons.
> Young women wanted to be Andromache,
> but how could they ever be? If any woman was born
> to be broken on the earth's turning wheel,
> I am she . . .

By fabricating the actress Irene Pappas saying these lines, I believed that my translation would depend on my ability to create a version that demonstrated both the simplicities and complexities of American speech and language, simplicities of statement and complexities of meanings—a tone of voice that established credibility by straight talk with overtones. So I invented the character in the opening speech by simulating her character until she emerged. What began as my invented version of Irene Pappas became, in the final version, Andromache. My voice as Irene Pappas' voice became

Andromache's voice. Sometimes I left the manuscript for a year before returning to it with what I felt to be new insights for attack.

I also knew that the choral speeches were not right, that as the opening lines were not explicit and innovative enough, the choral speeches were not formal and innovative enough. How to discover, how to innovate?

The key, as it always is, was tone, and the key to the key was to be form itself. Form was what I had to discover. I'm talking about language credibility, a tone established by innovative (meaning a form of the unexpected) explicitness, a precision elevated by suggestion, what Robert Frost called "words charged by ulteriority." This means form as arrangement creating implicative structures in the body of the larger work. To put it another way, form is language striving to solve language problems as it gives information, language as self-discovery, playing on itself, not as facility but as pattern that reveals more than itself.

What is revealed in this playing is the play itself, the character in action. The artist starts with the problem of craft being equal to the problem of precision and ends with the problem of craft becoming the problem of precision. The poetry is the play, the playing is the play, the masked characters are unmasked. In the original Greek performances, the characters were masked; so the language of the characters unmasked them. This unmasking comes about because of language, one that doubles itself in meanings, if the language is "working." For the translator, the problem is to invent language of self-discovery, but the hurdle is double: the literal meaning of an already discovered language plus the invention of another self-discovering language of accommodation (improvisation).

In the original composition to be translated, the poet is working from hunches, feelings, and fragments of ideas, sometimes tentative and groping, to a language of specifics that accommodate the trial draft. In translation, the translator/poet has the added burden of an already plotted sequence of actions and meanings which he or she must in some way couple into the process. Form is simply the hurdle the poet adopts to allow the language to discover itself. The poet, working to solve the "problem" of content, takes on the added problem of form, whether the form is free verse or any traditional form, in order to increase the potential of language. This is a difficult concept for the novice poet who feels constrained or burdened by the idea of form as something extraneous to the poem. Such burdened poets do not usually think of free verse as a greater burden because they do not realize that as form it demands an inevitability of line that is often more elusive to discover than one in a more recognizable and traditional form. Each free verse poem demands its free verse form, as inevitably as traditionally formal poems do.

Speech, of course, discovers its own rhythms. Great talkers rely on tone, timing, and imagery as truly as great writers do. In verse plays, the talkers talking poetry are doing it as if they were "merely" talking. When the verse dramatist successfully creates the illusion of conversation by crafting with the techniques of poetry, he or she heightens the effect of words. The character is clarified and humanized as his or her language is stylized, as that language emanates from a self-recognizing struggle to define him- or herself.

So the problem in translating the choral odes was the same problem: to invent a language in which form, given the literal meanings of the text, was the midwife. My earliest version of lines 268–291 went as follows:

CHORUS

Strophe

What suffering Hermes started
at the glade of Ida! The son
of Maia and Zeus drove a chariot
behind three goddesses yoked together,
their crested manes groomed
for a beauty contest, a grudge match
in front of the lonely cowherd
on his barren heath.

Antistrophe

The goddesses sped to the green groves
and bathed their glistening bodies
in the mountain streams; they threw
themselves past the son of Priam, fawning
flatteries. Aphrodite dazzled him
with words. She won him over
and doomed Troy.

Several years and versions later, the passage had become this:

CHORUS

Strophe

Oh what suffering Hermes began
at the glade of Ida, the son
of Maia and Zeus who drove
the three-fillied chariot of rival goddesses,
yoked together in splendor,
their crested manes groomed
for a grudge match of beauty
before the solitary cowherd
and his barren heath.

Antistrophe

When the goddesses came
to the forest-haired grove
and bathed their glistening bodies
in the mountain streams, they threw
themselves past the son of Priam,
fawning flatteries too sweet for mortal
ears. Aphrodite's sparkling sounds
of eloquence won the afternoon,
and days of misery for the Phrygian city,
the undermined towers of Troy.

Sixteen years after I began the translation, I took the manuscript to the island of Bimini in the Bahamas, armed with my original notes and three poetic and one prose published versions of the play. For two weeks I reworked the lines, trying to discover for the twelfth time a new version. I figured out that, although every passage in the play presents its own problem, what I needed most was a tone of voice that could accommodate both the lyricism and the weight of Euripides' meanings. My earliest mentor in the literal Greek of the play had requested that I listen to him reading the Euripides aloud in order to hear the original rhythms, but each time he did so I fell asleep. Although I wholly take the blame for my sleepiness, I had to come to terms with my own hunch that I would have to focus on the meanings and implications in the text and invent a tone and language that would produce its own rhythms. It was to be eighteen years later on Bimini where I discovered my tone and my final version.

The rhythmic weightings of the literal Greek were obvious to me, but how to solve the problem. The strophes I had written read like a list of drawers full of single images. As I worked the passages again, my solution became clearer to me as I tried to verbalize what Euripides was implying between the lines, rather than concentrate on what he was literally saying in the lines themselves. I also knew that this experiment would risk overstatement and flamboyance.

My struggle with the form of the passages finally yielded this:

CHORUS

Strophe

Passion is a cankerworm—
the trouble started on Mount Ida
when Hermes reined in his chariot
at a lonely grove,

the son of Zeus and Maia,
leading three golden goddesses
to a fatal test of beauty's disguise,
armed with glistening thighs,

to a herdsman's farm
where a young man lived alone,
warm by a hearth fire
far from harm.

Antistrophe

Under the grove of forest hair
the goddesses romped in spring-fed pools,
bathing golden lips,
bare bodies shining,

then through the trees, angling
toward Priam's son with fawning guile
and the dearest words,
competing in the promises of flesh.

Aphrodite did the trick
with her golden throat, and the boy,
heady with sweets, lay down under her golden net.
She toppled Troy to rubble.

It had occurred to me that, if I could find an interior image that would understate the yoking of passion and suffering, I might be able to bridge the gap between the conversational tone of choral imperative and its role as historical guide. Somehow, in one of those indefinable image/sound connections, I had in my mind a seemingly unrelated image from—Thomas Wyatt's poem "They Flee from Me." I could not get the word "guise" to go away. Perhaps it was the guise in "disguise"; I don't have any way to tell. But the seductive scene in Wyatt's room and the scene on Mount Ida became yoked together for me, even though Ida was an external scene and Wyatt's room an internal one. Passion became the link for me between the two, and I knew then that I had to create an interior feeling in the Ida scene. The word "cankerworm" occurred to me, and I yoked it with passion. Once the passion/cankerworm image occurred to me, I began the stanza, listening for similar sounds, internal rhymes and near-rhymes, to further the tone; hence "Hermes"/"reined"/"lonely" followed by "son"/"golden"/ "armed"/"glistening" and then "herdsman's"/"farm"/"man"/"alone"/ "warm"/ "harm." From "passion" came "Hermes"/"Zeus"/"goddesses," which lead to "disguise"/"glistening thighs." I was able to turn grove into a metaphor of hair and to eliminate a forced adjective. I substituted "romped" for "bathed," "angling toward Priam's son" for "threw themselves past," and "Aphrodite did the trick with her golden throat" for "Aphrodite's sparkling sounds of eloquence won the afternoon."

Back in 1974, when William Arrowsmith suggested that I might take on the *Andromache* as a translation project, I naively imagined it to be a hurdle easily jumped within a couple of years at the most. From my now educated perspective, however, I offer only the observation that what began as the

translation of a Greek play has somehow transformed itself into an opportunity to translate my own voice and life to myself. Whatever I have learned
about tone and its centrality in the creative process has become true in life
itself. Tone is the teacher. Attitude is where self-discovery begins, in the
playing of plays and in the playing of life.

Since beginning the translation of this play, I have run the Boston mara-
thon, spoken at my mother's funeral, cheered the birth of three grandchildren, caught a seven-pound largemouth bass, lucked out of a deadly gale
off the coast of Nova Scotia with no engine power, run with the bulls in
Pamplona, videotaped the Chinese 27th Army on R & R in the Forbidden
City three weeks after the Tiananmen Square massacre, and between times
carried the *Andromache* with me to Lincoln, Vermont; Freiburg, Germany;
St. Petersburg, Russia; L'Viv, Ukraine; Perugia, Italy; the Isle of Skye, Scot-
land; Xiamen, China; Bimini, Bahamas; Swan's Island, Maine; and Deerfield, Massachusetts. This modest odyssey, however, which seems to focus
on geography, has much more to do with the persons I have known in all
those places, from Lincoln, Vermont to my home in Deerfield. It was in
Lincoln that I sat up late at night in William Arrowsmith's farm library listening to him read his translations of Pavese's "Grappa in September" and
"Atavism" and "Simplicity"; then driving in his truck, just for something
to do even later at night on old Vermont roads, drinking beer; then the next
day walking across his hilly land, Bill talking all the time about Greek plays
and poetry and translations, and answering when I pointed and asked about
the flora: "Spirea," and smiling, meadowsweet in the Vermont summer air,
Andromache in the air, everywhere, for me. Bill later never liked any of my
versions. When he died I owed him a debt I could never pay the way I
wanted to.

I have other debts related to this play. My first mentor was Robert Dyer,
who prepared tapes for me when I was learning the Greek meanings of the
text for the first time. I am grateful to him for his expertise, his even tem-
perament, and his good cheer. My second mentor was Herbert Golder, who
deserves more credit for whatever felicities occur in this translation than I
can ever repay him for. Line by line, Herb taught me the text. His open
discussions with me and his uncompromising fidelity to Euripides and his
text were ultimately responsible for my being able to resist the temptation
to set aside the project. His dissertation, "*Andromache*: A Study in Theatri-

cal Idea and Visual Meaning," published after our collaboration,[2] is clearly the most thorough, cogent, articulate, and indispensable study of Euripides' *Andromache*. I owe a final, also unpayable debt to the late Tom Gould, who gave me invaluable help on the first 116 lines. I take complete responsibility for inaccuracies and indelicacies in my translation.

2. Dissertation, Yale University, 1984.

Cast

ANDROMACHE, widow of Hector and slave of Neoptolemus
SERVANT WOMAN
CHORUS of Phthian women
HERMIONE, wife of Neoptolemus and daughter of Helen and
    Menelaus
MENELAUS, king of Sparta, father of Hermione
MOLOSSUS, boy, son of Andromache and Neoptolemus
PELEUS, Grandfather of Neoptolemus
NURSE of Hermione
ORESTES, son of Agamemnon and nephew of Menelaus
MESSENGER
THETIS, goddess, once wife of Peleus
NONSPEAKING
    Manservant of Peleus
    Attendants
    Men bearing the body of Neoptolemus

(Neoptolemus' home in Phthia, near the altar of Thetis.
Andromache and a servant woman are speaking.)

ANDROMACHE
    O Thebe, Thebe! You were the shining face of Asia
    when I rode away on that caravan, a little golden girl
    riding her father's treasures to Troy, dowry
    for Priam, daughter for the palace hearth, for Hector to
           make sons.
    Young women wanted to be Andromache,
    but how could they ever be? If any woman was born
    to be broken on the earth's turning wheel,
    I am she. I watched my husband Hector die
    under Achilles' hands, and on that day
    the Greeks swarmed Troy,   10
    I watched my son flung from a tower—my son, Astyanax!
    And I—the daughter of a royal house—

packed off to Greece and bonded,
a plum for Achilles' son, Neoptolemus
the island prince. Andromache, his Trojan trophy.
Now I live here in Phthia with all these open grasslands.
Pharsalia, the nearest city, is just over there.
Thetis herself lived here at one time with Achilles' father,
away from the world—just Peleus and his Sea Goddess.
The people of Thessaly made this altar for Thetis,   20
they remember well her marriage here. This house belongs
to Neoptolemus, but Peleus rules Pharsalia. The prince
will never take his grandfather's crown until the old man dies.
Inside, I lay in the bed of Achilles' son
because he owned me, and I delivered him a son.
Even in my worst despair,
I hoped that if my son could stay alive,
he would eventually grow strong enough to save me.
Then Neoptolemus stopped coming to my slave's bed
when he married Hermione the Spartan.   30
The man who lorded over me gave me up.
Hermione has stormed ever since. She abhors me.
She says that Neoptolemus neglects her
because of me, that I'm some kind of witch,
drugging her and casting spells of barrenness over her,
that I'm trying to worm my way back
to Neoptolemus, to the bed Zeus knows
I had no stomach for when I was in it
and now have left forever. Hermione acts stone deaf
when I talk to her because she wants my throat in her hands.   40
Her father Menelaus has come from Sparta to help her in this.
Right now they are together in the house, making plans.
I'm afraid of them—
This altar, even this close to the house,
may save me. Peleus and all his family
treat it as a sacred shrine, remembering the days
when Peleus was married to the Goddess of the Sea.
Just now I hid my son in another house—he's my last son
and they would kill him if they found him here with me.

His own father cannot help us. He's in Delphi   50
apologizing to Phoebus Apollo for his hot-headed demands
that Apollo account for Achilles' death.
He is praying for Apollo's forgiveness, and for more time.
Neoptolemus yearns for Apollo to leave the future open.

SERVANT WOMAN

Lady Andromache—you'll always be Lady to me—
you deserve the same respect here that I gave you in the palace
in Troy. I loved you and your husband when he was alive,
and I'm still loyal to you.—
But I'm so frightened—someone may see me with you.—
I must talk to you. I know something.   60
Menelaus and the girl have woven a net—
I'm terrified for you and the boy.—
You must be so careful.

ANDROMACHE

Dear sister—now you *are* a sister in bondage
with your queen of other days—what are they planning to do?
Throw their net over this tired body? Then what?
Do they really plan to kill me?

SERVANT WOMAN

No—Lady Andromache, it's your son. They've found him.
They're going to murder him.

ANDROMACHE *(cries out)*

She's got Molossus. She tracked him down.   70
Oh dear god, how? She's got both of us.

SERVANT WOMAN

I don't know, Lady Andromache. I heard them talking,
then Menelaus disappeared. He's gone to bring the boy here.

ANDROMACHE

It's the end of it!—My son!—Those two creatures will kill you.
And they call him your father, still in Delphi!

SERVANT WOMAN
> Achilles' son should be here. None of this should be happening.
> No one is on your side in this. You need a friend, Lady
> Andromache.

ANDROMACHE
> What about Peleus? Have you heard anything at all?

SERVANT WOMAN
> That old man couldn't help even if he were here.

ANDROMACHE
> I've sent so many messages to him.   80

SERVANT WOMAN
> Whom did you send, friends?

ANDROMACHE
> I understand, yes—will *you* go for me?

SERVANT WOMAN
> Lady Andromache, how could I explain it if I left the palace?

ANDROMACHE
> Think! You're a woman. You can invent ways.

SERVANT WOMAN
> Hermione acts like a sentry. It's so risky.

ANDROMACHE
> You see? Even you back away from a friend who needs you.

SERVANT WOMAN
> Don't say that, those words sting—
> I'll go,

even if I pay later. It doesn't matter.
Women in bondage pay anyway.   90

ANDROMACHE
Go this second—hurry!
This is the bed of the dead. I could scream
to the hollows of the gods.

Women taste the bitter pleasures of rue on the tongue.
The very words of regret
sustain us hour by hour. This weight is worse
than anything I have known, my husband Hector wrung
                        from me,
my Troy in ashes. I am bound
in a web of shames that blackens every hour.
Don't ever say a woman is happy until she sees death itself.   100
Wait until the final moment of the final day
and you see her cross to the world below.

Inside the bridal rooms of the Towers of Troy a firestorm
smoldered in Paris' arms—not a bride at home
above the clouds, but Helen's body lusting, and Greek armies
unloading on Troy's shores, mobbing fire for fire with cries
of "Helen, Helen." Oh lovely Troy, Helen blackened you to
                        the ground,
and Achilles, the Sea Goddess' son, dragged Hector my husband
around the outside walls, a chariot's trophy—Andromache's Hector.
They dragged me from my bedroom to the mobbing shore   110
with a slave's hood on my head. I wept the tears
of eyes beholding a home in ashes, a city gone, a dear
husband with no face in the dust. Not Andromache, Misery—
now every day breaks on my bondage to Hermione. Tell me why.
I beg Thetis with my outstretched arms—deliver me.
I cannot stop crying—I am gushing inside stone.
                        Goddess! Sanctuary!

CHORUS

Strophe I

Woman of Asia—
you're keeping a long watch here
at the sacred knees of Thetis.
You will not leave her—   120
I am Greek, from Phthia,
but I come to salve your anguish,
and to try to stop the eruption
of blood talk between you and Hermione:
your dark feud over the double bed
of Achilles' son.

Antistrophe I

Think about your entanglement.
Face what it means! A daughter of Troy
cannot compete with a Spartan princess who owns her.
Leave this place where the Sea Goddess shines.   130
They sacrifice sheep here.
What good comes from a suffering that scars your soul?
The powerful get what they want. Power does it.
Give in. You are nothing to them.

Strophe II

Come away now. Leave this temple niche
where the Sea Goddess reigns.
Ponder your bondage on alien
soil, a city not your city,
no friendly faces anywhere to be seen.
You're a woman whose luck has gone.   140

Antistrophe II

Woman of Troy,
the sight of you stunned me with pity
when you came to this house.

I agonize for you now but I keep it to myself.
I am afraid of the granddaughter of Zeus.
I pray she never knows I befriended you.
(Enter Hermione.)

HERMIONE

Observe, all of you, these gold earrings, this gold crown.
Look at the embroidery in my gown—real gold flowers.
You think these are heirlooms from this house?
That they came from Peleus and Achilles? Ha! You're looking at
Spartan gold   150
from Laconia. My father Menelaus gave these to me.
You're looking at a sample of my dowry.
Understand one thing! I speak as a Spartan.
That is my *reply* to all of you—
(turns to Andromache)
And now *you*, the slave bitch—the war trophy
who wants to sashay through my house,
who thinks she can just throw me out.
You've done well. You've managed to poison my husband
against me
with your drugs. My belly is dry. Not one baby.
You barbarian women are good at these things.   160
You have the warped wits for it. But I'm stopping you right here.
You'll get no sanctuary from Thetis. You're going to die.
(pauses)
Even if a god or anyone else interferes here
you better forget your high-minded views
and lower your sights. If you have a future it's at my knees.
You're going to dazzle my floors—and from my gold pails
you'll sprinkle the waters of the Achelous River into every cranny
of my house, and scrub. You'll find out where you *really* are
without Hector,
without Priam and his stash of gold. This is *Greek* soil.
You poor fool, crawling into bed with the son of your
husband's killer,   170

making a baby for him. Well, you Asians know all about that.
Your fathers have sex with their daughters, sons do it with
                    mothers,
sisters with brothers. You people murder each other and call it
family squabbles, and you have no laws because you love it all.
You're not bringing those perversions here. It's sickening.
Just thinking of a man coupling two women in the same bed
turns my stomach. My god, if a man wants a good home
he should sleep with one wife who wants him.
One Aphrodite is enough for any man.

CHORUS

Women by nature fight for men, but it's worse   180
when a woman shares a bed with another woman.

ANDROMACHE

Being young is a kind of sickness,
    and it's deadly when the young are unfair.
(turns to Hermione)
Perhaps my bondage should temper my talking openly to you
even though what I have to say is true.
If I embarrass you with the truth about this household,
I know I'll pay for it. Those of you who breathe lofty air
don't have ears for the gods' truth spoken by inferiors.
But I'm not going to cower away from the truth.
So—can you explain, my fetching lady, what earthly reasons   190
might move me to desire your place in this house?
Has Troy's destiny been reversed? Is Sparta in trouble? Are you
                    standing there
looking at an emancipated woman with a sleek young body?
Am I dancing among the power and gaiety of my friends
singing the glories of Troy?—so I can walk back into your house
and take it over? Are you so worried that I can produce
a school of slave sons to swim behind me in my miserable wake
that some Phthian woman will raise my sons to be kings here

because you cannot conceive a child? Do Greeks here in Phthia
        love me?
Are they unaware that I was Hector's wife and Troy's queen?   200
Listen. Drugs of mine didn't turn your husband against you. The
        fact is,
he can't stand you. If you want to cast a spell on him,
try being fair-minded and pleasant. Forget your make-up.
Husbands respond to decency. But when anything upsets *you*,
you automatically compare it to Sparta. Skyros shrinks to
          nothing.
You strut with your gold here among much less fortunate people.
You inflate Menelaus at the expense of Achilles.
Of course your husband hates it.
A married woman should respect her husband even if she lives
        differently
than she's used to—not nit-pick. If you were married   210
to a king in the mountains of Thrace where the winters are long
and the men bed down a dozen wives, would you brand all the
        other women
insatiable and kill every one? This is so ugly.
Yes, of course women know what desire is,
it's a worse sickness in us than in men,
but we make the effort to conceal it.

(aside)

Hector, Hector—When Aphrodite turned your head,
I made friends with your other women,
I even suckled their children for your sake.

(to Hermione)

Yes—I did. Hector respected me for it.   220
But you're even afraid to let your husband step outside alone
in the evening dew. Your mother, dear girl, was always lovesick.
Don't compete with Helen. The daughter of an easy woman
should not imitate what she sees at home.

CHORUS *(to Hermione)*

My lady, if you can find some way to do it,
try to reach an understanding.

HERMIONE *(to Andromache)*
>You're so self-righteous! You *dare* to goad me with your
>>contentiousness,
>as if I'm the excessive one.

ANDROMACHE
>What you've said to me is not excessive?

HERMIONE
>I won't have a mind like yours in my house.   230

ANDROMACHE
>You're very young. You talk without shame about deeply
>>shameful things.

HERMIONE
>You talk so glibly about shame, but you do disgusting things that
>>hurt me.

ANDROMACHE
>*That* again. The drama of neglected passion.

HERMIONE
>Yes. Why not? Isn't passion the most important thing in a
>>woman's life?

ANDROMACHE
>Yes it is, if the passion serves the woman as it should. Otherwise
>>it pollutes everything.

HERMIONE
>How Eastern! We Greeks think differently about things.

ANDROMACHE
>Shameful things bring shame everywhere, in or out of Greece.

HERMIONE
Clever. Too bad you are going to die.

ANDROMACHE
Do you see Thetis looking at you?

HERMIONE
I see her despising Troy because her son Achilles was
                murdered there.   240

ANDROMACHE
Your mother did it, not Trojans—Helen caused Achilles' death.

HERMIONE
You keep at it. You keep digging where it hurts the most.

ANDROMACHE
No, I've said it. I close my mouth on all of this.

HERMIONE
Not until you tell me what I came out here to hear.

ANDROMACHE
I'll tell you one thing—you're mind is warped.

HERMIONE
Are you going to leave this protected place?

ANDROMACHE
If you promise not to kill me. Otherwise I'll never leave it.

HERMIONE
Then I promise I *will* kill you—and before my husband
                comes home.

ANDROMACHE
    I won't give myself up to you before he does.

HERMIONE
    Maybe I'll burn you out of here and be done with you.   250

ANDROMACHE
    Light your fire. The gods can see fire.

HERMIONE
    I'll carve your precious flesh. I know how to get at it.

ANDROMACHE
    Do it. Soak these stones with my blood.
    Thetis will follow you everywhere.

HERMIONE
    You're like an animal taunting me,
    daring me to kill you! You'll move—
    you'll jump eagerly from that statue.
    I have a little piece of bait. We needn't talk about it now.
    Your time is ripening, and you'll see.
    For now just squat right where you are. Even if you're fixed in
            molten lead,   260
    I can make you move before the son of Achilles returns.
    You think he's your great hope.

ANDROMACHE
    Yes, he is my hope.
(Exit Hermione.)
    This is a strange world—the gods have revealed balms and cures
    for all kinds of poisons, but no defense
    against a woman driven by demons. She's worse than snakes
            or fire.
    What a curse for humankind.

CHORUS

Strophe I

Passion is a cankerworm—
the trouble started on Mount Ida
when Hermes reined in his chariot   270
at a lonely grove,

the son of Zeus and Maia,
leading three golden goddesses
to a fatal test of beauty's disguise,
armed with glistening thighs,

to a herdsman's farm
where a young man lived alone,
warm by a hearth fire
far from harm.

Antistrophe I

Under the grove of forest hair   280
the goddesses romped in spring-fed pools,
bathing golden lips,
bare bodies shining,

then through the trees, angling
toward Priam's son with fawning guile
and the dearest words,
competing in the promises of flesh.

Aphrodite did the trick
with her golden throat, and the boy,
heady with sweets, lay down under her golden net.   290
She toppled Troy to rubble.

Strophe II

His mother should have thrown
the fatal child from his crib, before he could walk

the rock paths of Ida—
on that day beside the god-tongued laurel tree:
Cassandra screaming "Kill him!
His shadow darkens the face of Troy!"
dancing her dervish
around every elder, crying
"Kill that baby!"   300

Antistrophe II

Trojan women
would have eluded chains,
Andromache the queen
would rule at home,
Greece would never know
ten years of the Trojan wall,
ten years of cries
of young males dying.
No widow beds,
no old men sobbing   310
at the news
of dead sons.
(Enter Menelaus with Molossus.)

MENELAUS

Here's your son, home again. Apparently you misplaced him
in another house when my daughter wasn't looking.
Well now—you thought this Thetis statue would save you
and your, shall I call them, friends? But as it happens,
your mind is not as quick as mine. You must *realize*, I am
                        Menelaus.
Now—perhaps you should get away from that goddess statue.
I might have to cut the boy's throat instead of yours.
Think about it.   320
How you might die yourself if you prefer to save his throat.
Whichever. One of you will pay for the trouble you've caused my
                        daughter and me.

ANDROMACHE
    Limelight—
    a thousand nobodies swaying in front of bulging eyes.
(turns to Menelaus)
    I admire anyone who earns his rank.
    But the fakers who turn tricks on luck, the swaggerers, I despise.
    When their own luck turns, they are left alone with what
            they are.
    So now you. Are you really the one who came through our gates
            in glory?
    The commander of the fighting Greeks who grabbed Troy from
            Priam!
    You poor man.   330
    Are you out here all on your own
    or is your baby daughter keeping your nerve, lording it over
            a woman?
    I'm already in bondage,
    hero of Troy. You're not worthy to be a conqueror.
    Troy deserved more than you.
(turns away)
    Those who appear wise have an aura about them,
    but inside they're like everyone else. Unless they are wealthy.
    Money is so powerful.
(turns back to Menelaus)
    Menelaus, talk about this thing with me.
    What if your daughter does it, what if she actually kills me?   340
    Then the stain is on her, she's branded, and you're part of it.
    You'll stand charged with her.
    But if you kill my son instead of me,
    do you think his father will do nothing? Trojans remember
            Neoptolemus differently.
    He'll know exactly where to take revenge. He's the grandson
            of Peleus.
    Achilles was his father. He will pack your daughter out of
            this house.
    How will you explain *that* when you try to marry her again?

That she was too good for a worthless husband?
Truth finds its way out of a house. What man will marry her?
Or do you plan to keep her in the house until her hair turns gray 350
and her body all wrinkles? That's pitiful, and reckless.
Don't you see the tidal wave coming?
Wouldn't it be better if she put up with a dozen infidelities
then be disgraced or hidden away, alone?
This is a small thing between us. There's no need for a great
        explosion.
We women are curses of destruction, but men should not
        copy us.
What if I really drugged your daughter, as she claims, and she
        lost children—
let me stand before Neoptolemus and answer to him.
I'll eagerly leave this sanctuary to be judged fairly.
Neoptolemus will find me guilty if I took away his sons.   360
That's what I want to say, but I'm still afraid of that dark thing
        in you.
The last time you fought about a woman, you left the city of Troy
        in ashes.

CHORUS

Stop talking like that. Your thinking has gone wild.
You are speaking to a man. You've gone past the boundaries of
        your cause.

MENELAUS

Yes, woman. What's at stake here might be a small thing, as you
        call it.
Greece shouldn't be bothered by this. It's not worth a king's time.
But what you must get clear in your head is this: a man wants
        something
when he wants it. He wants it more than any Troy.
And if a woman gets shoved out of her husband's bed, it's
        serious.
I've locked arms with my daughter in this thing.   370

Most matters that women cry about don't interest me.
But if a woman loses her husband she might as well die.
My son-in-law has his rights with my slaves.
My daughter and I have our rights with his.
We're very close here. What we have belongs to each other.
There's no private property among real friends.
This situation doesn't require that I wait for anyone to return.
I'd be a damn fool if I did. My interest is right here now.
So you better jump, woman. Get away from that statue
or the boy feels the knife on his throat.   380
If you prefer the knife instead, he'll keep breathing.
Come on—one of you. Either one.

ANDROMACHE *(cries out, but quietly)*

You want me to draw straws for the knife at our throats?
You know that my son's death is my death, and mine his. Misery
          and death are twins.
Listen to me, Menelaus. You're dropping a mountain on me.
Why do you want to see my blood? How did I hurt you?
Whose country did I betray? Did I kill a child of yours?
Did I torch your home? Yes, I slept with Neoptolemus—for god's
          sake, he forced me.
Kill *him*. It was his bed. Don't forget how all this started.
For all of us, not just me. Why rage at me and not the
          instigators?   390

(turns away, cries)

My home, my country—all the beds of agony.
Why did I have to have another child?

(to Menelaus)

I saw what was left of Hector at the end of that rope behind
          Achilles' chariot.
I felt the heat of Troy burning. I felt them dragging me by the
          hair to the Greek ships,
Then I was on water. Then I was here in Phthia—then all
          the hands
handing me over to my husband's killers—for keeping.

Is there anything good left in life for me?
This? How is this any better than the past?
That boy is the last light of my life.
(to herself)

They are going to kill him. They decide who lives and dies.   400
I mustn't—what good is this body but to save him?
One chance can keep him alive.
If I don't take it, I'll blacken what's left of my life.
(to Menelaus)

Look. I'm leaving the Sea Goddess. You can have me.
Tie me up and hang me, or use your knife now if you want.
(to Molossus)

My son, my little boy, I'm standing up for us now,
then I will go to the underworld so you will be safe.
If you can run on your strong legs past today, think of mother,
how she hurt when she died. Tell your father how it happened
and kiss him on his cheek with your tears and hug him.   410
(to the Chorus)

Our souls are in our children. I have always known it.
Those without children may think they're lucky, but it's bad luck.
Without our pain, they never know the good fortune
            they missed.

CHORUS

Your words wet our cheeks with tears.
A foreign woman's suffering hurts us as our own.
Menelaus, try to fix things between your daughter and
            this woman.
Give her a chance to walk away from her troubles.

MENELAUS *(to Chorus)*

Grab her, ladies. Don't baby her. Use your arms.
She's not going to enjoy this—
(to Andromache)

I got you away from that statue, didn't I?   420
Dangling your son in front of your nose.

Coaxing you with this knife into my hands for a little
      blood-letting.
You *know* what your chances are. That leaves your son.
Maybe my daughter wants to kill him. I'll give him to her.
Crawl into the house. You've got a lesson coming in servitude,
from a master.

ANDROMACHE *(screams)*
    You lied to me. Everything was lies.

MENELAUS
    Why don't you blow a bugle about it? Of course I lied.

ANDROMACHE
    So this is the shrewdness you learned on the Eurotas River?

MENELAUS
    To the point. You Trojans know all about it. Hurt those who
        hurt you.   430

ANDROMACHE
    Because the gods are not divine, and do not remember justice?

MENELAUS
    We'll deal with the gods when the time comes.
    First I'll take care of you.

ANDROMACHE
    What about my boy you've grabbed?

MENELAUS
    My daughter can have him. If she wants to kill him, that's
        her business.

ANDROMACHE
    O my son, so soon and I am mourning you.

MENELAUS
  His prospects are not too good, in fact.

ANDROMACHE
  Everyone on the face of the earth hates Spartans—
  you twist things. You deceive people and you lie. You even
            deceive yourselves
  with your twisted view of things. In your minds you crowd out
            everyone else.   440
  Then you circle around, you encircle everything with schemes.
  Nothing is healthy. You spread Sparta like a disease.
  Greece knows how unjust and vile you are. What won't you do
            for power?
  Murder is trivial for you. Gold is a plaything.
  Your tongues bulge with deception as your minds scheme.
  Let the gods damn you. You seem to think death frightens me.
  You've already killed me twice. You wasted Troy, you killed
            Hector,
  my *husband* Hector who faced you down more than once,
  you, a puny skittering sailor who ran for his ship when Hector
            flashed his spear.
  Now you come at me like an infantryman. Look at you, rabid to
            kill a woman.   450
  I will not lick your hand or your daughter's hand.
  Hear my words: You are powerful now in Sparta, but I was just as
            powerful in Troy.
  If you put my body in this earth, be careful how you talk
            about it.
  You may come to the end of your loose tongue.
(Exit Menelaus, Andromache, Molossus, servant woman.)

CHORUS

          Strophe I

  Two double beds are too many for one man.
  Two mothers are too many for one son.
  Two double beds spawn hearts of stone.

A man should husband one woman
for a happy home.

Antistrophe I

In government it's also true: two sovereigns   460
cannot rule as well as one.
Double power brings
double burdens and public scorn.
Even the muse loves to pull strings
when two poets work on the same poem.

Strophe II

A young sailor holding one rudder firm
in a driving wind, can outsail a veteran helmsman
with a double-rudder boat.
A chorus of rival assemblymen becomes one
when a single statesman takes command,   470
even if he stutters. At home
and in the house of state
one voice in control is better than debate.

Antistrophe II

The firebrand Hermione shows us this.
The Spartan general's daughter burns
to kill her Trojan rival
and the little son. She's in a jealous
rage that provokes no laughter from the gods.
This killing is hideous.
Hermione, a turnabout is coming   480
in your direction.
Look over there. They're leaving the house
in chains, coupled together
for the killing. A woman
so miserable, and the forlorn child
to die for his parents' entanglings,
innocent of this trouble with the Spartan king.
(Enter Menelaus, Hermione, Andromache, Molossus.)

Strophe

ANDROMACHE

My wrists bleed
from these chafing chains.
I am going below the earth.   490

MOLOSSUS

Mother! Mother, I am beside
you. I am going too.

ANDROMACHE

This is sacrificial murder,
you rulers of Phthia.

MOLOSSUS

Father, please
come home to us.

ANDROMACHE

Soon you will rest,
my lovely son, forever,
next to your mother's breast.

MOLOSSUS

Mother, I'm afraid. Where can we go?   500
What are they going to do?

MENELAUS

Let's go, the two of you, down under. I hate your looks
and your city. Your fates are decided. We took
a vote on each of you. Woman, I voted to kill you.
My daughter Hermione, your son. Only fools
let enemy sucklings crawl around their floors
when they can step on them and rid the house of fear.

Antistrophe

ANDROMACHE
> O Hector—
> we need you standing here, spear in hand,
> Priam's son, my husband!   510

MOLOSSUS
> It seems so dark here.
> Maybe I could sing a song
> to push away the wrong.

ANDROMACHE
> Pray, little son.
> Hug the knees of the strong man.

MOLOSSUS *(hugs Menelaus at the knees)*
> I want to be friends.
> Please don't hurt me.

ANDROMACHE
> The tears of my eyes—
> how cold my face,
> a dark rock spring of misery—   520

MOLOSSUS
> O sir! Can you help
> me go around these troubles?

MENELAUS
> What are you doing pawing at me?
> You might as well kneel at the edge of a tidal sea.
> I'm as hard as a granite ledge.
> I help my own people. There's no way I can include you.
> I've already given up too much of my life
> bringing Troy to its knees and dealing with Hector's wife,

your mother. You can thank her
down under.   530

CHORUS
   Over there! Peleus is bending toward us,
   hurrying his ageless legs.
(Enter Peleus, with a manservant.)

PELEUS
   What is this? Open your mouths. Whose blood is this?
(calls to Menelaus)
   Ah, General Butcher, what are *you* doing here?
   Why is this place a madhouse? Who let you suspend the law?
   Stop right there, Menelaus. Not another step without authority.
(to his manservant)
   Help me. Damn these legs. This is not the place to relax,
   I can see that. I need the old power to steady me.
   A good shot of my youth would do it.
   First I'll blow some wind into this courageous woman's
                             sagging sail.   540
(to Andromache)
   Speak up. What are they accusing you of,
   chaining both your arms and wrists and pushing you around
                             out here?
   A ewe and a lamb bound for slaughter
   when my son and I are gone!

ANDROMACHE
   They took us, old one. You can see what they did.
   We're on our way to the underworld. What else can I say to you?
   I sent you letters . . . surely my fear . . . letter after letter,
   Some word must have reached you of the turmoil here.
   This house is torn apart. Hermione's claws are on my head.
   She blames me and wants me to bleed for it. She pulled me from
                             the sanctuary   550
   without a trial. I thought I was safe with the goddess Thetis,
   your own son's mother whom you adore, but they came at me

before you and Neoptolemus could return.
I had no help and they knew it. Oh god, Peleus, Molossus should
                    not be part
of this business but they're pulling him down with me.
For god's sake don't let them kill us.
These chains cut both ways. Without them I could touch
                    your face,
to beg you. Help us, Peleus.
If we die, we'll die in pain,
and our bodies will leave a stench in this house.   560

PELEUS

Loosen those chains before I make one of you cringe
like this boy. Get those couplings off her wrists.

MENELAUS

Hey you! Don't move!
(to Peleus)
I've got as much jurisdiction here
as you have. More, as far as she's concerned.

PELEUS

Tell me how you decided that. Because you goosestepped here
                    and took over
my house? Because Sparta can't help oozing all over the earth?

MENELAUS

I'm the one who took her at Troy and brought her back.

PELEUS

She was a gift of war to Achilles' son.

MENELAUS

My slaves are at his disposal for the asking. Surely his belong
                    to me.   570

PELEUS

For proper treatment, not to manhandle and kill.

MENELAUS
  Get one thing straight. You'll never take her out of my hands.

PELEUS
  Do you think this staff on your head will enlighten you?

MENELAUS
  Touch me with it! Take another step!

PELEUS
  Ah, so this is how to be a manly son of Atreus? You squirt.
  How the hell could you even be a number in that house?
  You lost your wife to a little Phrygian boy.
  You *presumed* she would be loyal, instead of the itchiest slut of
        them all,
  so you left your bedroom doors unlocked—
  not even a sentry outside the house.   580
  What Spartan woman could resist?
  Spartan girls can't play it straight if they want to.
  They walk out of the house in short skirts like young men.
  They love to show their thighs at the stadium, running
        and wrestling
  with the boys. Pretty uninspired stuff.
  How can you be so caught off guard when your women prowl?
  Didn't Helen teach you anything when she ran off with an
        adolescent boy
  to a foreign country? Helen, the expert on family ties!
  For her you mustered armies of Greeks and rallied them
        against Troy?
  You should have bribed the Trojans to keep her.   590
  But not Menelaus. You didn't even think about it.
  You smelled the blood of innocent young men and sent them
        hell bent
  into the blood-letting, and left old women to doddle in
        empty houses,
  and old men to daydream of lost sons.

I'm one of those old men.
You're polluted, Menelaus.
I hold you responsible for Achilles' death.
You were the only unscathed Greek at Troy.
You brought home polished shields in unscratched leather covers.
I warned my grandson about diseased mares   600
before he married into your family.
One affliction begets another.
(Listen, you suitors: study the daughter's mother.)
But there's something else:
how can you live with your sacrilege against your brother
                    Agamemnon,
wheedling him to butcher his daughter for a small change
                    of wind?
You who clutched your gonads when your voluptuous wife
was missing, then when you finally broke into Troy
(that's right, I'm going all the way),
you didn't even think about killing her when you got your hands
                    on her,   610
not you. Those dipping breasts of hers were too terrific to
                    pass up.
You unbuckled and dropped your sword and puckered all over,
bellying up for that cunt. You poor sap.
Then you come to my grandson's house when he's gone
and put your grubby hands all over the place,
actually try to kill a decent woman and her child
who not only belongs here, but who will repay you and
                    your daughter
for all of this. This little bastard boy!
Yes, beware of *him*.
A little bit of good topsoil can outproduce a worn-out field—   620
and an illegitimate son can outshine one from a legal marriage.
Get your daughter out of here!
An honest union with good in-laws
is a hell of a lot more meaningful
than a fake relationship with a ship of rich fools.
You poor fool.

CHORUS
>The human tongue turns talk
>into trouble. Men who know better
>should guard against clashing with friends.

MENELAUS
>Who says old people talk wisdom   630
>or that Greeks from the old days are shrewd?
>You, Peleus, from a noble family,
>my own kin by marriage, talk such rubbish
>and shame all of us, for an Asian woman!
>You should have dumped this woman on the other side
>of the Nile, way beyond the Phasis River.
>And you should have asked me to help you.
>She's an Asian. Those people cut down the manhood of Greece
>and left a pile of rotting corpses over there.
>Your own son's blood is on her hands.   640
>She's the wife of Hector, Paris' brother.
>Everyone knows that Paris killed Achilles.
>And you let her flounce into your house
>and eat at your table.
>Then you sit around while she proceeds to have a baby.
>They're our *enemies*, man.
>Here I am trying to help you
>and you jump to pluck her right out of my hands.
>Think for a second. No harm in thinking, right?
>Let's say that my daughter can't have children   650
>and this one buds babies all over the place,
>what are you going to do with them, make them kings?
>You want barbarians ruling your country?—telling Greeks what
>   to do?
>Am I stupid for holding the line on basic things?
>You call your own position reasonable?
>Think about something else.
>If you married your daughter to a fellow Greek
>and he abused her, would you keep quiet about it?

Of course you wouldn't.
But for a goddamned Asian you carp at me,   660
your own relative. It's hard for everybody when a marriage sours,
especially for cheating. That poisons men and women.
But a man can fix those things with his own hands.
A woman has to go to friends, or to her parents.
Hermione's my daughter. Why shouldn't I help her?
I think your years are getting the best of you.
What you say about me being a general
actually supports my view of this thing.
I'm glad you brought it up.
Helen got into trouble because the gods fixed it that way.   670
It wasn't her doing at all.
But it turned out to be the best thing for Greece.
Greeks were totally innocent of weapon-skills and combat.
Then young men rubbed shoulders with other young men
and learned what it's like to be *real* men.
Experience! Yes—Helen.
True, I did restrain myself when I met my wife face to face,
but I was actually being very prudent. It was a moral decision.
In fact, you would have done better to behave as well,
instead of killing your brother Phocus.   680
I offer these suggestions to be helpful, not to prick you.
If you get all hot-headed, you'll just wear out your tongue.
My policy is, precaution pays.

CHORUS

Stop this talky-talk! The best thing now
is to stop saying words that hurt each other.

PELEUS

What a sham that we decorate generals
after our armies hang their spears from trees in triumph.
Foot soldiers deserve the battle markers on the fields,
not the fathead general who raises his spear over his head later

in front of the crowds, taking credit for ten thousand braveries.   690
That flatulent lounger in the statehouse. Nincompoop!
Ordinary citizens have his number.
Ordinary citizens know. The difference between them is that an
                    ordinary citizen
doesn't have a general's mendacity.
You and your brother, sitting all puffed up near Troy,
a mile away from the action,
watching that crusade of young boys suffer and bleed
for each other! You've got another lesson coming
if you think that Ida's prince Paris was less trouble for you
than I am—back out of here,   700
now! Pack your sterile daughter with you
before my grandson drags her out of the house by the hair.
Your dry little troublemaker can't stand for other women
to have children. Just because she's an unserviceable cow,
our family should go without grandchildren?
Get *away* from her, you fool slaves.
We'll just see who tries to stop me from loosening these chains.
Here, lift up. Yes, I'm trembling. These double links are twisted
                    so tight.
Now, one's coming.
You bastard! Her hands are all bloody and cramped.   710
Big man chaining a bull! Maybe a lion?
What were you afraid of, that she'd pull a sword and run
                    you through?
Crawl over here, son. Here, duck under my arms
and help me work that set over her shoulders.
I'll bring you up in this house right here in Phthia.
You'll show the Spartans what an enemy is.
They're so bloody famous for shiny swords at the turn of a battle,
but when you take away their weapons, they're nobodies.

CHORUS
    Old men can go haywire
    when their tempers flare. They go right out of reach.   720

MENELAUS

You go too far. You're being abusive.
I didn't ask to come here to Phthia and I don't want to force
                any issue.
But no one's going to force me either.
So for now—actually, I don't have any more time here.
I have—there's a city, fairly close to Sparta, in fact,
it used to cooperate with me, but it's making trouble.
I have to put some troops together and put things back in
                order there.
When I tidy everything the way I like it,
I'll come back here and talk to my son-in-law in person.
We can exchange views.   730
If he halters this woman as she deserves,
and shows the right attitude toward me in the process,
I'll reciprocate. But if he blows up,
I will too. I'll match his nastiness to his regret.
All your ranting doesn't faze me.
You're pathetic. You're only a shadow of a man.
All you can do is mouth words.

(Exit Menelaus.)

PELEUS

Here, little fellow, stop trembling. That's it, under my arm.
You too, woman, come on. You ran into a storm,
but the harbor's quiet now.   740

ANDROMACHE

God keep you and your whole family, old man, you did it.
My son and I were their targets for sure, and we're both
still breathing. But please keep watching. Those men know
the woods around here, and they know your age.
They can easily grab us again. I have no defense against them,
and I've got this baby boy. You must be so careful.
We're free now, but tomorrow we could be in their hands.

PELEUS

    No more woman talk. Keep walking.
    Who's going to touch you? Anyone who dares
    will wish he hadn't. The gods like me in charge here   750
    in Phthia. I've got a good cavalry and plenty of foot soldiers.
    And don't think I don't stand tall enough for this, I'm not
            feeble yet.
    Never mind my age. Whoever touches you will bolt
    as soon as I look at him. An old man who knows his strength
    can handle plenty of younger men.
    What good's a trim body if your heart fails you?
(Exit Peleus, Andromache, and Molossus.)

CHORUS

    Strophe

    If I couldn't be raised in an aristocratic home
    with the means to live right and well
    I'd rather not be born at all. When bad times come,
    only families of honor have abundant means.   760
    Whoever enters the world from a noble home
    carries the prestige of performed deeds.
    Nothing can steal reputation, not even time.
    Excellence survives death, and generates fame.

    Antistrophe

    A victory which celebrates
    dishonor, stains the use of violence
    in behalf of justice, and creates
    hate. Malice makes no sense.

    Such a victory turns sweet sour
    in its time; revilement hangs dead   770
    in a barren house. Fairness is our
    mandate, in government and in bed.

Epode

Old man Peleus, son of Aeacus,
I know you fought with the Lapiths
against the Centaurs. Long ago
you crossed the Treacherous Mists
beyond the Dark Ledges on the Argo,
that voyage forever sailing into time.
Even before then, when Heracles threw the net of blood
over ancient Ilium, you equaled   780
the very son of Zeus in fame,
and brought it all the way home to Greece.
(Nurse enters.)

NURSE *(to the Chorus)*

Oh friends—dear sisters! It's bad inside.
Every minute it gets worse. The mistress
(I mean Hermione) was left alone by Menelaus
and started to brood about her awful attempt to kill
Andromache and the boy, and now she wants to kill
herself. She's terrified of Neoptolemus.
She says he will throw her out of the house
for what she did and everyone will know it.   790
She thinks he might even kill her for plotting
against his war trophy. Her servants have just pulled her
from a noose, and wrestled a sword from her hand.
Her guilt is killing her. She knows how bad
her plan was. Dear ones, I'm exhausted
just from trying to keep her alive. I beg you
to go inside and try to talk her out of this.
Try to save her. Maybe new friends
can help her more than an old one.

CHORUS

Listen! We can hear the servants screaming.   800
It sounds as bad as you described.

She seems about to show us her grief
for what she tried to do. Here she comes
running from the maids, slipping from their hands.
She brings a passion for death.
(Hermione enters, running.)

Strophe I

HERMIONE

Oh dear god! Dear god! I *will* tear out my hair!
I'll gouge this face with these fingernails!

NURSE

Child, why are you doing this?
Tearing your own body?

Antistrophe I

HERMIONE *(screams)*

What good is it? I'll fling this hair net   810
up! There! Webs!

NURSE

Child, cover your breasts. Do up your dress.

Strophe II

HERMIONE

What are breasts—
what can I cover up with robes now?
Everything else is uncovered. My husband will see it all.

NURSE

Are you so sad because you tried to kill the other woman?

Antistrophe II

HERMIONE

Sad? For god's sake, woman,
do you know what remorse *is*?

Yes, I'm sad! I'm also finished.
I tried to kill her.   820
I'm cursed. I'm cursed for everyone.

NURSE

Surely your husband will forgive your mistake.

Antistrophe

HERMIONE

Give me back that sword!
Why do you keep taking it from me?
Give it back. Oh nurse, please
give it back to me. I'll push it here,
in my breast. Where are you going with that noose?

NURSE

Child, do you think I'm going to let you do this?
You're so beside yourself.

HERMIONE

Kind death!   830
I'll find a pyre of lovely flames—
Someone help me to the cliff above the trees—
near the ocean rocks—down—
to the sea, into the dark woods. Only the dead can care for me.

NURSE

Why are you doing this, Hermione?
In time, divine trouble comes to us all.

HERMIONE

Father, O Father, you left me here alone.
You walked away from me on this empty beach,
the sea stretching away with no oars.
My husband will kill me. My god, he's *going* to.   840
I can't live any longer in his house. My bridal house.

What god's statue can I run to? Do I have to cringe
like a slave at another slave's feet?
(changes her mood suddenly, almost sings)
     If only I could be a gray-blue bird, oh to fly Phthia—
     a pine hull with Jason, sailing by the Blue Cliffs
     to the end—I see—the first ship's sails!

NURSE
     Try to hear me, child. You're so headstrong. You jump
     into things. You flew at the Trojan woman, now you're flying
     at yourself. Come to your senses. Your husband
     will not disown you because of a barbarian woman's tongue.   850
     You're not a souvenir from the Trojan war.
     You're a distinguished general's daughter
     who sent you here with a lavish dowry from a substantial city.
     Hermione, your father knows you're here, don't be afraid
     that he's abandoned you. He'll never let anyone drive you
     from this house. No more now—come inside.
     Come on—good. Any more spectacle
     and people might think there's a scandal.

CHORUS
     Look over there! Someone is coming fast.
     He's wearing foreign clothes.   860
(Orestes enters.)

ORESTES
     Women of Phthia, this honored roof—does the son of Achilles
          live here?

CHORUS
     Yes he does. Tell us who you are.

ORESTES
     I am the son of Agamemnon and Clytemnestra,
     called Orestes. I'm traveling to Dodona,
     to the oracle of Zeus. I have a relative in Phthia,

and I want to find out if she's in good health, and happy.
She's my Spartan cousin. Her name is Hermione.
Sparta is a long way from here, but she's very dear to me.

HERMIONE

Oh safe harbor! Orestes, it's you,
dear Agamemnon's son. These waters have been troubled   870
for this sailor, but I'm on my knees to you
now to take pity. You can see my despair,
these arms around your knees. Take them
as the arms of prayer.

ORESTES

What is *this*? Can I believe what I see?
Is this the queen,
Menelaus' daughter?

HERMIONE

Orestes, it's *I*! Did Helen have another daughter
in Menelaus' house? You *know* me!

ORESTES

Apollo!—Healer! Bring help here.   880
(to Hermione)
Who did this to you, a man or a god?

HERMIONE

Some of it's my fault, Orestes, but also my husband's,
and a god's involved. I'm ruined.

ORESTES

What could be wrong for a woman with no child,
unless there's trouble in her marriage?

HERMIONE

I'm sick inside all of it. You've said it.

ORESTES

    Is there another woman? Might your husband be . . . ?

HERMIONE

    Hector's bitch, his Trojan trophy.

ORESTES

    That's ugly. One man and two women.

HERMIONE

    It's been my life here, so I fought back.   890

ORESTES

    You didn't take the woman's way? You didn't try to harm . . . ?

HERMIONE

    I planned to kill her and her little bastard of a son.

ORESTES

    Did you get it done?

HERMIONE

    Old Peleus got involved and sided with the scum of the family.

ORESTES

    Did anyone help you in the murder plan?

HERMIONE

    My father rode from Sparta. He was helping me.

ORESTES

    And the old man turned him out?

HERMIONE

    He respected the ancient creature. Then he walked out on
             all of it.

ORESTES
I can see it all. Now you're afraid of your husband for what
you did.

HERMIONE
Yes I'm scared.   900
I know he'll kill me, and with reason.
What else is there to say?
Oh, Orestes, in the name of Zeus our family guardian,
take me away from here, get me as far as possible from this place.
Take me home to my father. This house is pounding inside
my head.
The whole country of Phthia despises me.
If my husband comes back now, finished with Apollo
and the oracle, he'll deal with these charges and he'll kill me.
Or I'll be a slave to that demon woman I used to control.
I know everyone's talking. They're asking how I fouled it all up.   910
I'll tell you. I listened to sly women slink around here
and flatter me. My head was a sponge for their frothy talk:
(*mimics the women*)
"Why do you allow that awful captured slave
to sleep with your husband?"
"By the Queen of Heaven, she wouldn't lounge
between my sheets and stay alive!"
I listened to the wagging tongues of these sirens
mouthing their hen talk and their poisons,
and I got puffy with vanity. Why *did* I act like a sentry
in my husband's own house? I had it all.   920
I had lovely things. I controlled the nest.
I could have had legitimate children
to rule her little bastard slaves.
But *never, never, never* should a man with any wits
let other women gossip to his wife in her home.
They get to the heart of real trouble and they fire it.
One wants to tilt the marriage so she can move in,
another is into her own trouble and wants a companion.

There are always nymphomaniacs around.
That's how a man's home goes rotten.   930
(to the Chorus)
        Guard your doors. Put locks on your bolts and keep
                        predators out.
Women don't cross your thresholds for their health.
They have nothing on their minds but misery and stealth.

CHORUS

        You're talking too freely about the problems of women.
        I understand, but women who talk about women's excess
        should sand the edges of female wickedness.

ORESTES

        The god who advised us to get both sides of a story
        knew what he was doing.
        I knew about the blowup here,
        the whole thing between you and Hector's wife.   940
        I've been listening to it from out there with my spies.
        I waited to see whether you'd stay or be scared off
        by your faceoff with Andromache. I knew you had cornered her
        and she got away. I came despite your letters telling me not to.
        I thought if we could talk like this
        you'd give me a reason to take you with me. Once,
        you were *my* wife. The only reason you live with this man
        is because your father talks double. Before Troy
        he gave you to me, but as soon as Neoptolemus threw in with
                        the war
        Menelaus promised you to him if we won.   950
        I kept my temper with your father. I understood his deal.
        But when Achilles' son came home I pleaded with him
        to give up his claim on you. I told him about our family trouble
        and my own problems, how the goddess trailed me day
                        and night,
        how my only chance for a marriage was within our own family

because of my exile for murder. He berated me
for killing my mother. He taunted me about the goddesses
        following me
with their eyes oozing blood.
He humiliated our family and made me feel like a reptile.
I hurt deep inside myself for all that had happened   960
so I went away without you, cheated.
Now they're telling your fortune and trying to make it come true.
I'll take you and put you in your father's hands again.
Family bonds are strange, but they're true.
If you're in trouble, it's best to be with a relative.

HERMIONE

My father will decide about our marriage.
I can't make that decision.
But let's get *out* of here
before Neoptolemus catches up with me
or Peleus hears I'm running out   970
and comes after us on those young horses he drives.

ORESTES

Don't be afraid of an old man,
and forget your fear of Achilles' son.
He's gouged me for the last time. I've already got the stage set
for him. A nice little death-web he won't wriggle out of.
Enough said about it. The Delphic Rock will show it all.
So I'm a mother-killer!
If my boys in Phthia keep their blood vows to me,
he'll know what a mistake it was to take my woman.
He'll get a bigger return than he expected   980
for demanding Apollo pay him for Achilles' death.
Guilt feelings won't get him out of it
when he pays his last respects.
This finger will point him out, and the fate will cut him down.
He'll feel my revenge in his bowels.

The gods hand over the fates of men they hate
to upheaval, and crush presumption.
(Exit Hermione and Orestes.)

CHORUS

    Strophe I

O Phoebus Apollo,
who towered Troy on that hill of walls—
O Poseidon, lord of waves,   990
who whips gray-blue horses over the sea,
what anger drove you
to ruin your creation?
why did you hand over Troy
to the frenzy of Ares,
spear crazy, murderous—
why did you abandon Troy?

    Antistrophe I

Herds of horses, throngs of men
on the sandbanks of the Simois!
Grinding chariots to bloody death—   1000
where are the laurel wreaths?
The princes of Troy are gone.
The altars of Troy are damp clods,
the fires out, the murky smoke gone,
the altars empty of incense, the smell of the gods.

    Strophe II

The son of Atreus is dead.
God the Death-Trader demanded twice-red hands,
and the killer son killed the killer wife.
Clytemnestra paid with her life
when the son of Agamemnon heard the god cry out her name   1010
in his Delphic chamber. At home

in Argos he murdered his mother. Her body's outcast
returned death for death. Phoebus, how can I believe this?
(Peleus enters with Andromache, Molossus, and attendants.)

Antistrophe II

In the marketplaces of Greece
women mourn dead
sons. Widows sleep
in strange beds
with new husbands. A disease
weighs down the earth. You
are not the only one who grieves.   1020
All Greece grieves. A tornado
whirled through Troy
leaving Hell's gore on every seed.

PELEUS

Ladies, I need to know the exact truth.
I heard some talk
that Menelaus' daughter left the house
and rode off. I came right over.
When a friend is away
those of us here have to hold things down.

CHORUS

Peleus, you heard it accurately.   1030
It would be wrong of me
to hide our problems. The queen left the country.

PELEUS

What did it? You can tell me.

CHORUS

She panicked that her husband would throw her out of
the house.

PELEUS

So her plot against his son festered?

CHORUS

Yes, and she was afraid of the woman brought back from the war.

PELEUS

Did she go with her father or somebody else?

CHORUS

Agamemnon's son took her home with him.

PELEUS

What does *he* want? Is he going to marry her?

CHORUS

Yes he is, and he's going to kill your grandson.   1040

PELEUS *(whirls around)*

An ambush or a fair fight?

CHORUS

A Mycenaean and a gang of Delphians in the shrine of
       Loxias Apollo.

PELEUS

My god—this is bad! Will someone—you!
Ride for your life to Delphi, to the temple.
Tell any friends you can find what's happening.
Fly! before the son of Achilles is murdered.
(Messenger enters.)

MESSENGER

An awful, awful thing, old man!
I've come to tell you, and all my sadness speaks.
I have to hurt you with my message, and all my master's friends.

PELEUS

O god, my heart—say it!   1050

MESSENGER

Old man, your grandson is dead.
The Delphians and a Mycenaean stranger
hacked him to pieces with their swords.
(Peleus starts to go down.)

CHORUS

Not this too! Old man, don't fall.
Here, get to your feet.

PELEUS

My life is over—I can't say the words—
my legs—

MESSENGER

If you want to help your friends, stand steady,
listen to what happened.

PELEUS

Moira! Daughter of Destiny! I'm at the boundary   1060
of this life, and you still torture me.
(turns to the Messenger)
You can tell me. My only son's only son! Tell me
the one thing I thought it would kill me to hear.

MESSENGER

When we reached the historic plain of Phoebus Apollo,
we spent three whole days sightseeing, marveling
at everything, sunrise to dusk.
We were under suspicion from the start.
The sanctuary attendants huddled in little groups,
gossiping about us. Meanwhile,
Agamemnon's son stalked every circle   1070

of men in the city, pointing to us and whispering,
"Do you see that man?
Every day he paces the golden shrines,
eyeing Apollo's treasuries and offertories again.
The last time he came,
he ransacked the temple clean."
Waves of ugly excitement surged across the city,
officials filed in and out of council chambers.
Even the treasure keepers posted their own guards
between the temple pillars.   1080
All this time we knew nothing,
and took sheep from the pastures of Mount Parnassus
to the steps of the sacrificial altars.
We were standing with our sponsors and the Phthian priests,
and one of them said,
"Young man, what shall we ask of the god for you?
Why did you come to Delphi?"
Neoptolemus said,
"I wish to make amends to Phoebus Apollo for a blunder.
Once I demanded that he pay me for my father's death."   1090
Soon it became clear that Orestes' lies had worked.
The priests were thinking that Neoptolemus was the liar.
He crossed into the stairwell to pray before the oracle,
and started the offerings.
Right there behind him, disguised by laurel branches,
a gang waited with drawn knives.
One of them was Orestes, Clytemnestra's son,
who wove the whole scheme together.
Neoptolemus was praying in open view before the god,
without a shield or protective armor,   1100
and didn't see them.
They rushed him with their knives and stabbed him.
He reeled back, not fatally cut,
drew them near the armor pegs
and grabbed a shield and a sword off the vestibule wall.
He leaped to the altar, glaring at them
as if looking through a helmet's narrow slits,

shouting to the Delphians,
"Why are you trying to kill me?
I came here in reverence! 1110
What do you think I've done?"
Hundreds of men gathered around, not saying a word.
In total silence they started throwing rocks.
Neoptolemus thrust his shield here and there
but it was a blizzard and he couldn't stop it all.
Then arrows flew at him, and thonged javelins, and
                pronged spits.
Ox pikes clanged around his feet.
You should have seen your grandson, old man,
warding off those shots,
doing the Pyrrhic war dance. 1120
But they shortened the circle around him,
and he needed breathing room.
He sprang from the altar stone with the great leap of Troy,
kicking down at them, charging them.
They turned their backs and scattered like doves under a hawk.
The dead and wounded crammed the exits,
some were crushed in piles.
Men's screechings reverberated off the stone walls of the temple.
My master stood unmoving, brilliant in his armor,
and everything was peaceful for a moment. 1130
Then an incredible scream surged from the depths
of the inner sanctuary, strangely tortured,
and the aroused mob turned to fight again.
The son of Achilles fell,
a Delphian sword in his ribcage,
one of tens thrust at his chest. He was down,
and they went for him with steel and heavy stones,
mangling his flesh.
His lovely body was unrecognizable,
and they dragged it through the incense-clouded shrine, 1140
far from the holy altar, and threw it outside.
Then we took him in our arms and brought him here
directly to you, old man,

to anoint with your tears and your sorrow,
and to bury with honor in the earth.
Apollo, lord of oracles,
judge of justice for the world,
sentenced Achilles' son to Hades as he sacrificed.
The god held his grudge like an ordinary man of hate
remembering an old scar.   1150
Who can call Apollo wise?
(Messenger exits to join a group of men approaching with the body
of Neoptolemus.)

CHORUS

Look there, the prince is coming home from Delphi.
They carry him high.
You can see he felt the pain. It's your pain now, old man.
Achilles' son returns to a different end
than you could ever plan.
The blow that struck him down
strikes you down too.
(Neoptolemus' body is carried in.)

Strophe I

PELEUS

Oh God, no! what a wrong thing to have done!
My eyes to see this—ease him into the house—   1160
Oh Thessaly, Thessaly!
It's gone. The family
is finished. Our bloodline—
my son, my grandson—done!
This sorrow in my home—
To whom, where, can I open my eyes—?
(turns to the body)
Dear, dear boy—your mouth, your cheek, these hands—
if only a god had taken you at Troy, on the sands
of the Simois.

CHORUS

> Then death would have honored him, old man, 1170
> and your life would still be open.

Antistrophe I

PELEUS

> Sad marriage! That marriage leveled my home
> and brought my city down. Oh son!
> dear boy, our family made a bad bargain
> for children and an heir—Hermione is an evil name.
> Your bed together was a bed of death.
> She deserved a lightning bolt, not your hearth.
> Oh mortal boy, if only you hadn't accused Apollo
> of draining your father's blood with Paris' deadly arrow!

Strophe II

CHORUS *(with traditional movements of mourning)*

> Begin the sorry measure, begin 1180
> the mourning of the prince,
> the song of the dead.

PELEUS

> I, too, take up your chant,
> the sorry measure of an old man
> mourning, weeping.

CHORUS

> The gods stake out the final lots. This at our feet is what they do.

PELEUS

> Dearest boy,
> our house is empty.
> You have left me
> old, with no sign of a child. 1190

CHORUS

> You too should be dead. You should have died before
>> your grandchild.

PELEUS

> This old hair snaps at the roots!
> These fists crack against my brow!
> Oh hollow city! Apollo
> has stolen my two sons.

Antistrophe II

CHORUS

> Old man, you have known
> the pain that breaks the human
> heart. How can you start another life?

PELEUS

> I don't have a child in the world.
> Nothing can help that. Sadness breaks over   1200
> the last sunset.

CHORUS

> Your good marriage fortune that the gods foretold turned bad.

PELEUS

> My luck soared,
> then fell to ashes
> and dust, with all my boasts.

CHORUS

> You're alone in a house of empty rooms.

PELEUS

> My city's gone—everything of a gone city—
> even my staff—
> *(lets his staff fall to the ground, turns to the statue of Thetis)*

Daughter of Nereus, deep in your ocean caves,
you can see I've fallen   1210
in ruin.

CHORUS

Look up there! Look!
The air shimmers like fire! The heavens!
Look women, see it!
Something threads its way through the shining air.
It's coming over the pasture fields of Phthia.
It's lighting down!
(*Thetis enters.*)

THETIS

Peleus, it is I, Thetis.
I have come from the palace of Nereus
because of our marriage vows.   1220
In this agony you feel, do not despair.
I, who never should have known the white pain of grief
for a dead child, lost the one I carried for you,
our son Achilles with the swift feet, the pride of Greece.
Listen why I've come to you now.
Take the body of Achilles' son to the altar at Pytho
and cover it with the earth of Delphi, to their shame,
and to the shame of Orestes and his savage crime.
The tomb shall proclaim it.
As for the woman in bondage, I'm talking about
                    Andromache now,   1230
her destiny lies in the land of Molossia,
where she will marry Hector's brother, Helenus, who will
                    protect her.
She must take this boy with her, the last trace
of your father Aeacus. Kingdoms will stem from him
and will carry our own bloodline with Troy's,
unbroken to the end of time, despite Troy's
crumbling at Pallas Athena's whim.
Peleus, so you may still honor our marriage,

I give you eternal life. I am a goddess
and the daughter of a god. You will walk with an
                    upright carriage,   1240
a god, free of mortal sickness.
We will live forever in the palace of Nereus,
a god and a goddess together.
There you shall step dry-footed from the sea
and visit our lovely son Achilles
home forever at his gleaming Cape of White Sand
in the Blessed Islands of the Black Sea.
But first go to Delphi with this body
and bury it in the earth of the divine city.
Then return to the Sea Caves at Sepias   1250
to our old hollow, the hogback ledge you know,
and wait for me. I will come for you
out of the waves with fifty Daughters of the Sea
to guide you home. You will live the eternity
Zeus foresees. Do not agonize for the dead.
The gods decided long ago,
man's destiny is to die.

PELEUS

Daughter of Nereus,
goddess of my bed, what you are going to do
honors you and your children.   1260
I'll stop agonizing now, as you command.
When I have buried our grandson,
I will go to the glens of Pelion
where I once took you in my arms.
(Thetis exits.)
Shouldn't a man marry into a noble house,
and give women in marriage to wellborn men,
if he has sense?
Mismatches are the worst mistakes,
even if the dowries are huge.
(Exit Peleus, Andromache, and her son.)

CHORUS
>The gods shift and shape the world.　　　　　　1270
>They give and take the dearest things,
>twisting human lives for their own ends.
>A goddess clears the way for the unexpected.
>This is how it always ends.

The Bacchae

Translated by
Daniel Mark Epstein

Translator's Preface

When he heard that Euripides had passed away at the age of seventy-five, his old rival Sophocles was busy rehearsing a tragedy for competition at the Athenian Festival of 406 B.C. Sophocles was ninety. It is said that the author of *Oedipus Tyrannos*, in a show of respect, sent his chorus onstage in mourning dress.

The brotherly gesture cost Sophocles very little, and bought a great bounty of posthumous attention for the poet whose career the public had slighted and nearly forgotten. Sophocles had won the prize for tragedy no fewer than eighteen times while Euripides had received it only four. Comedians like Aristophanes ridiculed the younger playwright for his religious skepticism and his unconventional politics.

Euripides died far from Athens. Perhaps it was ill-treatment at the hands of critics that drove him from his home town in 409, at the age of seventy-one, or perhaps it was domestic troubles—the playwright was twice unhappy in marriage. First he went to Magnesia in Thessaly, where the city fathers received him as an honored guest. Then, at the invitation of King Archelaus, Euripides went to live at the royal court in Macedon. The Hellenizing king had gathered around him several poets, sages, and artists. In that company the old tragedian at last enjoyed the respect and convivial appreciation he had long hoped for in the hectic, war-weary city of Athens.

During the last two years of his life there in the fresh mountain air of Macedon, the poet wrote three plays: *Alcmaeon at Corinth* (lost), *Iphigenia in Aulis*, and *The Bacchae*. Most scholars, including Goethe, John Chapman, E. R. Dodds, and Paul Roche, consider *The Bacchae* Euripides' finest tragedy, "unmatched by any," according to the late William Arrowsmith, "except the very greatest among ancient and modern tragedies. You have to go to the *Oedipus Tyrannos* or the *Agamemnon* or *Lear* to find anything quite like it."[1]

---

1. Arrowsmith, *Euripides V* (Chicago: University of Chicago Press, 1959), p. 142.

The play has a number of features that set it above other Euripidean tragedies. The chorus is as fully integrated into the play's action as any major character; there is no *deus ex machina* arriving at the end to interfere with the course of events and spoil the play's integrity. The God, Dionysus, disguised as a mortal priest, is not just a remote presence in the play, he is the major character, the protagonist. So in this play Euripides has a special advantage in dramatizing his religious ideas, for he has created a world in which God and man interact convincingly. The dramatic action, absorbing and rapid from the first moment, and rising to a pitch of surpassing horror, is perfectly continuous and unified.

Soon after the death of Euripides, his son (or nephew) staged a production of *The Bacchae* at the festival in Athens. This posthumous drama was generously received and applauded—perhaps because the tone for its reception was so kindly prepared by old Sophocles the previous year when he dressed his chorus in mourning. So *The Bacchae* won the prize for tragedy that year, too late for Euripides to glory in it but not too late to give his reputation a second wind, a new life.

Competition between great spirits, in life and death, is a stubborn thing. We may wonder what Sophocles felt and thought of this mysterious, demonic spectacle, the bloody *Bacchae*, which a hostile audience might understandably have booed into oblivion but instead embraced. They would go on applauding, gasping, and weeping over the play down through the centuries, until Euripides' productions outnumbered Sophocles' by two to one, and then five to one, after Alexander's death, when Greek culture and Greek theater spread all over the known world. Three hundred and fifty years later, after the defeat of the Roman army at Carrhae in 53 B.C., *The Bacchae* was playing as far away as the Parthian court (now Iran), and the severed head of the Roman general Crassus was delivered to the theater just in time to be mounted on top of Agave's ivy-bound staff.

What a show! Who could compete with it?

Sophocles would not live to see the fame of the renegade Euripides virtually eclipse his own reputation and that of his idol Aeschylus, but it would happen. And Sophocles might well have had intimations of that rising sun, as he heard the driving rhythms, the colorful, tempestuous choruses of *The Bacchae*, high-stepping on the stage in 405. Nothing like it had ever been seen. Euripides' *Trojan Women*, for all its lyric beauty and pathos, had not been so much a play as a pageant of horrors. Only the *Medea* had shown as

well in the amphitheater, and it was so upsetting to the prejudices of the
Athenian citizens it received only a third prize. For one jealous moment,
Sophocles may have wished he had not dressed his own chorus in black,
resurrecting the career of the forgotten playwright.

In 1943, the scholar E. R. Dodds observed that no play of Euripides has
been as much discussed as *The Bacchae*. He might have added that no Greek
tragedy other than *Oedipus Tyrannos* has been so frequently translated and
performed. At last count there were seven English translations listed in
Books in Print. And these do not include the widely performed versions of
Gilbert Murray and the late William Arrowsmith.

Do we need another translation of *The Bacchae*? To speak at once for this
play and all the Greek tragedies: times change, our language changes, and
the language must keep up with the times. It's a long way from 406 B.C. to
the present, from the ancient world to twenty-first-century America. And a
Greekless reader who tries to view that ancient culture through the increas-
ingly distant lens of a dated translation, Elizabethan, Victorian, or Nixonian,
must find the translation almost as much an impediment to true understanding as the Attic Greek.

To speak more directly of *The Bacchae*, the theme of this shocking play
makes importunate demands on both translator and script, testing one's
response to fathomless differences in *mores* between the ancient world and
the modern, and to nuances in the two languages evoking those *mores*. It is
a time-sensitive theme, easily distorted by changing tastes and prejudices,
by the mercurial climate of opinion.

The Bacchae shows us the conflict between Pentheus, Prince of Thebes,
and the new God, Dionysus. Pentheus returns from a journey to find that
his city has been turned upside down by this strange God of wine, who leads
packs of women to revel in the hills of Cithaeron, where they indulge in
ecstatic "orgies." Pentheus declares war on the Bacchantes, denying their
God and his priest, who we soon discover is Dionysus in disguise.

Pentheus is the guardian of the State. He is the protector of law and order:
these depend on reason, and on good citizens living safely within their
senses. Dionysus is the irrational energy that inspires humankind, the animal instinct that makes humans one with Nature. Dionysus is the force that
drives men and women to ecstatic heights, in drinking, dancing, hunting,
war, and sex—and always in praising the God. Properly understood, all
these pleasures are forms of devotion, ways of prayer.

The theme of *The Bacchae*, the struggle between cold reason and emotional ecstasy, is universal and simple when applied to the individual. But the way history reflects the conflict—in revolutions, persecutions, and religious revivals—is extremely complex and difficult to convey. It is easy enough for an armchair philosopher to talk of "eternal verities" and tell us that human nature does not change. But the playwright and the translator do not deal in generalities, they deal in hard facts, concrete details and specific situations.

One does not render a milieu in generalities but in the poetry of things. It may please the structural anthropologist to say we are like the ancient Greeks in our essential human desires, fears, and spiritual concerns. But is it really true? At the end of the fifth century B.C., generations of war and militarization had led to such a strict ordering of public life in some Greek city-states that many people felt stifled by the rule of reason. They yearned for a greater indulgence in beauty and pleasure, a more intimate connection with nature. The reaction in Delos was the cult of Dionysus. Mobs of men and women drank themselves out of their senses, went running on the hills hunting wild animals, tearing them apart, and eating them alive, before settling down to more wine-drinking, dancing, and sexual free-for-alls in the forest.

All this, mind you, was done in a fervent atmosphere of religious devotion to the God. And this was not the eccentric behavior of a few outlaws but a broad-based religious revival tolerated if not sanctioned by the state.

Are we like those ancient Greeks who sanctioned the cult of Dionysus? No. The strict social conformity and political witchhunts of the Eisenhower era gave way to the ecstasies and excesses of the 1960s. Yet we did not hunt in packs and eat wild animals alive on mountain paths, nor were our ecstasies religious, for the most part. There were many pseudo-religions and many false gods during the Vietnam War, but these were not sanctioned by the majority.

If Americans want release from what Blake called the "mind-forged manacles," most of us do not seek it in Nature. These days, a more serious challenge to rationalism—in numbers and respectability—is the revival of fundamentalism in America. At the end of this century, the fastest-growing segment of Christianity is the "charismatic" movement, which values the emotional, ecstatic experience of union with Christ above the cooler rationalism of denominational Protestantism. But these charismatic Christians do not glory in the flesh. Unlike the ancient Greeks, most Americans deny the human body and the natural world as sources of mystical redemption; they distrust any ecstasy outside the walls of a church.

So the translator's main challenge is to render the ancient Greek conflict in contemporary terms. This is a humbling task. We are flawed mirrors of history. The Victorian translator whose choruses echoed the Presbyterian hymnal was doing his best to render the Bacchants' piety in contemporary language; so was the scholar of the 1950s who made his women choristers drawl with accents of existential irony. Now both of these scripts seem dated, counterfeit, quaint. We want, on the one hand, a certain purity of diction, a timeless flow of images and rhythms that the years will not betray. On the other hand we want the freshness of a voice rooted in the present, in the real world—in short, *in history*. Hence the paradox: the best translation must sooner or later become dated. The more concerned the play is with manners and customs, the sooner that translation is likely to spoil. Renderings of *Medea*, largely concerned with the personality and psyche of the protagonist, will last longer than *The Bacchae*, which relates a social upheaval in arcane religious terms.

I wished, in 1968, that Peter Brook would stage a version of *The Bacchae* with sex, drugs, and rock and roll, reflecting the decade's conflict between reason and passion, order and ecstasy. It did not happen. And now I think that if it had such a version would not have survived the deaths of Janis Joplin and Jimi Hendrix.

I have approached *The Bacchae* as a masterwork of the theater. So I have striven to write lines for actors to speak and audiences to hear, words that are always the manifestation of character in action. Scene by scene I have sought to maximize and clarify dramatic situations while keeping as close to the literal Greek as our English will allow. Translators, like scholars who interpret *The Bacchae*, do the author an injustice when they attribute to Euripides various motives and intentions not clearly set forth in the verses. They upset the play's moral balance, which is the narrative achievement of a mind so fine, as T. S. Eliot would say, that no idea could violate it. Euripides had ideas, and he may have had religious faith, but in this play he does not allow either faith or reason to dominate his dramatic structure.

Insofar as the play has a moral, it is obvious: the man who denies the force of Dionysus, the irrational, the ecstatic—the man who defies the

God—will bring ruin on himself and his people. But many scholars since the early nineteenth century have taken sides for and against Pentheus. They have come out for or against Dionysus, in favor of civilization or religious faith, in favor of reason or ecstasy—all depending on the historical moment and their own prejudices. And where the scholars lead, the translators are sure to follow.

Let me just mention a couple of wrong turns that readers of this play might as well avoid. For most of Euripides' writing life he expressed a lively skepticism of religious belief. So, one of the oldest and most popular readings of *The Bacchae* calls it a palinode or apology of a one-time atheist who in old age has got religion. This might make sense, if Euripides had not painted the God as so ruthlessly cruel to the naive Pentheus and the God's followers as so foolish and ultimately pathetic. The playwright's harsh depiction of the Dionysic cult has given rise to another, more cynical group of scholars. These see the play as a satire of the Bacchic mysteries, a cautionary tale meant to defend civilization against religious fanatics. This, too, is wrong-headed. The tone of the choruses everywhere assures us that the religious passion in the play is authentic, deeply felt.

What we are left with is a criticism of life, human nature, and civilization shown in such equipoise that neither can appear perfect, wholly wise, or blameless. We need reason and organization to live together in peace; we need passion and ecstasy in order to maintain our unity with God and nature. Neither is sufficient, and the two together can never exist harmoniously. For the brief time and space of this play, Euripides has held these contrarieties in solution; the playwright has given us the perfect balance of forces, protagonist and villain. It is such a moral balance that makes the most fascinating theater, and which, in the end, tells us most about ourselves.

ANNOTATIONS

I have used Gilbert Murray's text and *apparatus criticus* of 1913 with its commentary by E. R. Dodds.[2] Line numbers refer to the present edition, with the numbers of the Greek text in parentheses.

2. *Bacchae/Euripides*, ed. and intro. E. R. Dodds (Oxford: Clarendon Press, 1960, rpt. 1987).

7–13 (6–12). A place struck by lightning was believed to be charmed, an intersection of the natural and supernatural worlds.

81–84 (78–79). The orgies of Dionysus are closely associated with those of the Asiatic Cybele.

90–99 (88–98). The myth of the double birth, in this case the second birth from the thigh of Zeus, is mentioned in Herodotus and depicted on Greek vases and in other works of art. The tale also appears in the Indian myth of Soma, the Vedic god of wine. The Upanishads relate how the gods put Soma in the right thigh of the sky-god Indra. So it appears that the myth of the double birth is of common Indo-European stock.

99 (100). Dionysus is often depicted in Hellenist and Roman art as a young man with the horns of a bull.

99–103 (101–4). Snake-handling was once a feature of Dionysiac ritual, as it has been in Pentecostal services in various regions of the United States. Snake and serpent imagery figures heavily in *The Bacchae*.

107 (108). *mílaki*: bryony—actually *smilax aspera*, an evergreen creeper with white flower clusters.

118 (115). It is believed that the Bacchanalian orgy was originally a women's rite, with one male participant.

122–34 (120–34). Myth has it that the *túmpanon* was invented by the Corybantes in a Cretan cave; its noise was supposed to drown out the crying of the infant Zeus so his father, Cronus, would not find him and eat him up.

123 (123). *trikóruthes*: imaging plumes on the dancer's heads, I have translated this as "crested," though *trikóruthes* means literally "with triple helmet." No scholar has ever been able to determine what, precisely, is meant.

289–93 (292–94). Dodds suggests that more than one line is missing after *éthike tónd' hómeron ekdidoús*, rendering the fate of the *méros aithéros* ("piece of ether") uncertain.

291–95 (292–97). These lines depend on a play of words for which there is no equivalent, a pun on the words *méros* and *hómeros*. So I have substituted the more general paraphrase: " . . . the real child he spirited off somewhere so safe and secret it might / as well have been Zeus' thigh . . . Years pass, and the truth gives way to myth, / and so the story got garbled." While this is true, and preserves the continuity of the speech, it is not a translation of Euripides' verses 292–97 but an interpolation.

330 (334). *katapseúdou kalōs*: This is not a "noble lie" but one which makes a good impression.

361 (367). There is a pun here on Pentheus' name *Pentheùs* and the word for sorrow, *pénthos*. See line 491 (508).

394–96 (406–8). The "strange river" is probably the Nile.

449–50 (467–68). Pentheus is ironically suggesting that Zeus is not the father of the new god.

520–24 (537–41). I have followed Hermann and Dodds in striking out line 537, *hoían hoían orgàn* ("What rage, what rage he shows") as being an interpolation. The snakeman Echion was one of the men who grew from the dragon's teeth sowed by Cadmus.

525–26 (544). Giants are traditional figures of hubris.

556–80 (576–615). For most of the play I have had the chorus deliver their lines in a single voice, though directors should feel free to assign speeches to individual chorus members ad lib. But in this scene I strongly recommend that speeches be assigned as I have indicated, in order to realize the scene's full dramatic potential.

628 (652). Here a line, or lines, have been lost. I have given this line to Pentheus, imagining his ironic response to Dionysus' praise of the god in line 627.

629 (653). Literally, "What you try to condemn Dionysus for what is in fact his glory."

637–38 (661–62). This is poetic license on the part of Euripides. There is not always snow on Cithaeron. Snow was somewhat eerie to the Greeks, so Euripides might have thought a snowy landscape a fit setting for the marvels of the scene he is about to describe.

695 (725). *Íakchon*: "Lord of Cries," an Athenian and Eleusinian epithet for Dionysus.

696–97 (726–27). Dodds notes that *pān dè sunebákcheu' óros* "is quoted in the *de sublimitate* as an example of imaginative boldness verging on extravagance."

179 (751–52). These are towns among the northern foothills of Cithaeron; the herdsmen would pass them on their way to Thebes.

729–30 (761–64). It was widely believed that the worshipers of the god, when inspired, were invulnerable.

737 (767). *haîma*: not their own blood, of course, but the blood of the ruined cattle.

749 (780). This gate guarded the southern entrance to Thebes from the road to Cithaeron.

764 (795). Literally, "Don't kick against the goad, a mortal against a deity."

916–17 (945–46). Like the mad Heracles (*Her.* 943ff), Pentheus has delusions of superhuman powers. Dionysus humors him.

949–50 (977–78). *Lússas kúnes*: hounds of Lyssa. These are like the hell-hounds of that hunt with Hecate, and are reminiscent of Actaeon's dogs.

1061–63 (1084–85). Dodds: "Stillness is the traditional response of nature to a divine epiphany."

1088 (1114). Agave figures here as a priestess, *hieréa*, as Pentheus is doomed to be the victim of a sacrifice, *sparagmós*.

1148–49 (1173–75). Here the text is damaged, the restoration conjectural.

1148 (1185). Modern scholars translate *móschos* as "young bull," but the older tradition of translating it as "lion's whelp" is more consistent with the dramatic dialogue.

1178 (1198–99). *Megála kaì phanerá*: Agave here uses the same language the chorus employed in describing the joys of Dionysiac worship in line 986 (1006).

1222–80 (1244–98). Goethe so admired this recognition scene that he translated it into German as a "touchstone," representing the highest achievement of Greek drama.

1283 (1301). The answer to Agave's question: "Were you able to put him together at all?" is lost. Dodds says that there are probably three lines missing here, for which I have substituted Cadmus' response, "It's a sad sight . . . "

1315–60 (1329). Here the Palatinus manuscript is missing at least 50 lines, probably caused by the loss of a leaf or half-leaf of a medieval manuscript from which the Palatinus was copied. Information about the lost passage has been gleaned from a twelfth-century text called the *Christus Patiens*, a drama about the Passion of Christ that "collages" lines from *The Bacchae* and other Euripidean tragedies, and from a third-century description of the play by Apsines, a Greek rhetorician. For my reconstruction of the last verses I am indebted to E. R. Dodds and Gilbert Murray, and to William Arrowsmith, the translator who pointed the way by assembling the fragments from the *Christus Patiens* and various papyri in meaningful order.

1361–69 (1330–39). One of the thrills of reading Greek literature is also one of its chief frustrations: there are always a few passages so bizarre they defy comprehension. This is one of them. It is common for Euripidean

tragedies to end with a forecast or prophecy like this, but the specific mythology here, the dragons and snake-tribes and so forth, seem to belong to
a later culture, so that scholars have been inclined to consider this passage
an interpolation. I find the imagery aesthetically consistent with the Bacchic
snake-handling references earlier in the play, as well as the dragon ancestry
of the house of Cadmus.

1405 (1371). In Greek this sentence is unfinished, cryptic. Aristaeus was a
god of hunters and herdsmen. There is good reason to suspect a lacuna of
several lines here.

1420–24 (1388–92). The play's choral tailpiece is the standard moral ana-
pest that may also be found verbatim at the end of *Alcestis, Andromache,*
and *Helen,* and in slightly different form in *Medea.*

Cast

DIONYSUS (also called Bacchus, Bromius, and Evius)
CHORUS of Asian Bacchae
TIRESIAS, the aged prophet
CADMUS, founder of Thebes, grandfather of Pentheus
PENTHEUS, king of Thebes
SERVANT
FIRST MESSENGER, a cowherd
SECOND MESSENGER, from Cithaeron
AGAVE, mother of Pentheus, daughter of Cadmus
NONSPEAKING
    Attendants

*(Thebes, in front of the royal palace. The city is off to the right; to
the left lies the road to Cithaeron. Far upstage the backdrop
depicts the smoldering ruins of the tomb of Semele, mother of
Dionysus. Dionysus enters, a beardless, handsome young man
with long, curly hair, dressed in a fawnskin and carrying a
thyrsus, or wand tipped with ivy leaves.)*

DIONYSUS
    I am Dionysus, the son of Zeus. My mother
    was Semele, the mortal daughter of Cadmus,
    whose labor a flash of lightning cruelly sped.
    But I have shed the God's shape and come as a man
    to this land of Thebes. And thus you see me here
    by the springs of Dirce and the stream of Ismenus.

    Over there you can see my mother's tomb, near
    the house she lived in, where the lightning struck her.
    The ruins still glow from Heaven's deathless fire,
    and Hera's outrageous vengeance upon my mother.   10
    I praise Cadmus for making this place a shrine

to his daughter's memory. I made sure the grounds
are greenly shaded with the cluster-bearing vine.

I have traveled a long way, from the gold fields
of Lydia and Phrygia, past Persia's sun-drenched plains
and the walled towns of Bactria. From the stormy land
of the Medes to blessed Arabia I pressed on, through
all of Asia lying along the salt sea's coast.
Many a town have I seen, with beautiful towers
and Greeks and Barbarians mingling in the streets.   20
Everywhere I stayed to teach my dances and rites,
making my Godhead known to all men. But this
great city is the first I've reached in Hellas.
The Thebans are the first Greeks to take up my cry
of joy, put on the fawnskin, shake the thyrsus,
the ivy-bound spear I hand out. Thebes first—for here
my mother's sisters (who should have known better)
denied that Dionysus was son of Zeus.
They said Semele, pregnant by some mortal lover,
charged Zeus with sin she'd known between the sheets.   30
This was Cadmus' bright idea, they said, which caused
Zeus to slay her for lying about the affair.
These are the women I've worked into a frenzy
and driven from their homes to roam the hills,
out of their minds. I have forced them to put on
the garments that suit my orgies, every last female
seed of Cadmus' stock I have driven out, raving.
They sit on rocks with no shelter but the pines,
Cadmus' daughters, dally with anyone they please;
They know nothing of real Bacchanalian mysteries.   40

I must defend my mother's name—I'll show these mortals—
this city must learn, willing or not, the child
my mother bore to Zeus is a great God! Now,
Cadmus has given over the reins of power

to Pentheus, his daughter's son. He's waging war
against the Gods, as far as I'm concerned:
He pushes me away from his libations and never
mentions my name in his prayers. For these slights
I will show him and all of Thebes I am truly a God.
When I have set things right here, I will move on   50
to another land, until my divinity is known to all.
And if Thebes, in a vain fury against my Bacchae,
takes up arms, tries to drive them from the hills?
I will lead my army of Maenads into battle.
For this, I have taken on this mortal form,
shedding God's shape awhile to seem like a man.

Now let the revels begin! You women of Tmolus,
Lydia's rock wall, show us why you left home
so far away, to follow, serve and keep me company.
Beat those native drums of Phrygia mother Rhea   60
and I made, drum up a rhythm as you surround
the royal house of Pentheus. Let the whole city
of Cadmus see you! Meanwhile I'm on my way to Cithaeron
glen to join my Bacchants in their dancing.
(Dionysus exits as the Chorus comes dancing in from the right, dressed in
fawnskins and playing on flutes, cymbals,
and drums.)

CHORUS
From the land of Asia I come flying
over Tmolus' sacred ridges
to do this joyful work of the rhythm-King,
God's work, so easy, praising the Bacchic Lord.

Who's standing in the doorway,
who's blocking the road? Spread the Word,   70
get moving, and not a word of faithlessness.
Sing out the old-time hymns of Dionysus:

Oh, happy is the man
whose fortune it is to see
into the heart of Heaven's mystery.
Happy the ones who can
live their lives in purity,
whose souls know the Bacchic revels,
the dancing upon the hills
that frees us of our sins.   80
He knows the great mother Cybele's
orgies, and waving the thyrsus,
head crowned with ivy greens
he worships Dionysus.
Come Bacchae, come on,
and bring the God Bromius,
the son of a God, down from the mountain
and lead him through the Greek streets.
Bring our God home to us!
His mother gave up her life   90
as the lightning bolt of Zeus
struck while she was in labor.
To hide the child from his wife,
Zeus found him a new womb:
He stitched him up in his thigh
with golden pins. The jealous eye
of Hera herself could not find him.
And when the Fates had formed him,
Zeus delivered this bull of a God. He
crowned him with a crown of snakes   100
which the Maenads hunt eagerly
now, armed with thyrsi, snakes
to wind through their flowing locks.
Oh Thebes, Semele's nurse,
put on your crowns of ivy,
bloom with star flowers,
bloom with the green briony.

Be crowned with boughs of oak and pine
in your Bacchanal ecstasy.
And put on your dappled fawnskin   110
trimmed with tufted white wool.
Swing that reckless wand in
a spirit wild, yet worshipful,
so to make the whole world dance
when Bromius leads his band
of revelers to the mountain,
leads them away to the mountain
where throngs of women have come,
yanked from shuttle and loom
in the frenzy for Dionysus.   120

Oh, the Curetes' hidden sanctum,
Oh, the chambers of Crete where Zeus
was born, where the crested Corybantes
in a cave made me this drum,
this circle of stretched oxhide.
They put it in Rhea's hand
to back up the sweet accents
of Phrygian flutes in the band,
a crash of rhythm for the joyful Bacchants!
Then Satyrs took up the drum   130
from the Mother Goddess,
Now it's ours to keep the rhythm
every third year, in these dances
honoring Dionysus.

Oh, what joy on the mountain
as one strays from the revel-rout
and crouches low to the ground
in a holy robe of fawnskin.
He springs for a goat's throat
to drink its blood, make a sweet   140

meal of the raw meat
before rushing to Phrygia
or the Lydian mountains
after the Bromian Tiresias, shouting
"Eeyo!" Now earth flows
with milk and wine and honey;
Syrian incense fills the air.
Bacchus ties a pine torch
to his thyrsus to light the way
and he's running here and there   150
waving that flaming brand
and inciting stray votaries
to riot, crying aloud
and rakishly tossing his hair,
raising up his voice to be heard
by all the reveling crowd:
"Come on, you Bacchants, girls
of Tmolus, the land of gold, come
with your fetching Phrygian accents
and sing and dance to the drum   160
thundering, sing in praise
of the Evian God whose presence
makes us happy so many ways."
When you hear the sacred melody
of the flute, playful and sweet
and feet start to move with the beat
then it's time for the wild Bacchants
like foals in their mother's sight
in a field, to get up and dance.
(Blind Tiresias enters, dressed in fawnskin, crowned with ivy, and
tapping his way with the thyrsus.)

TIRESIAS

Pardon me! But is there someone at the gates   170
who is not so busy he couldn't help a blind man?
There is a fellow named Cadmus, the son of Agenor,

lives nearby I think. He came from Sidon
and founded this town of Thebes. Please, someone,
go and tell him I am here—Tiresias. He knows
why I have come. He will recall the pact we made,
we two old men, to take up the thyrsus, put on fawnskin
and crown our heads with ivy—
(Cadmus enters from the palace, dressed like Tiresias.)

CADMUS

                    My dear friend!
I was just inside the door, and was I ever happy
to hear your voice! Oh such a voice, the wise voice   180
of a wise man! As you see I am all ready, dressed
as the God would have me. For we must do him honor.
After all, he is my own daughter's son, and comes down
to show his divinity to men.
                    I'm ready. How shall I dance,
Like this? Like this? Shall I shake my old gray hair?
What do you say? Oh, Tiresias, old man, be my guide;
the old can lead the old, if one is wise. I swear
I will never tire of whipping the ground
with the thyrsus, day and night!
This ecstasy will make us forget that we are old.   190

TIRESIAS

Here! I feel the years recede. Just watch me dance!

CADMUS

Then, to the mountains? We'll take a chariot.

TIRESIAS

No, no. That won't do honor to the God.

CADMUS

We'll walk then. Come. The old shall lead the old.

TIRESIAS

    Let God lead us both! He knows the way.

CADMUS

    Wait. Are we the only men in Thebes to follow Bacchus?

TIRESIAS

    We understand him . . . others . . . misconceive.

CADMUS

    No more dawdling, come and take my hand.

TIRESIAS

    There, you have it, hold on tightly now.

CADMUS

    I'm only a man. When God speaks, I must listen.   200

TIRESIAS

    Indeed! Nor should we pretend to know too much
    about the ways of Heaven. Our fathers' faith, as old
    as time itself—no logic shall overturn it, no!
    Not arguments of keenest ingenuity. Now, someone might say:
    "Has this man no respect for his own gray beard,
    going off to caper with vine leaves on his head?"
    I say the God wants homage from us all, invites us all,
    the young and old alike, and the more the merrier.

CADMUS

    Blind Tiresias, I will be your guide,
    sharing my vision, repaying light with light.   210
    Now, Pentheus is hurrying toward the house, Echion's son.
    I've turned over the whole government to him.
    He sure looks frightened. I wonder what's on his mind.
*(Pentheus enters, leading attendants, all in traditional Greek dress. At
first he does not see Cadmus and Tiresias, but
delivers his speech to the audience and attendants.)*

PENTHEUS
    I was away from Thebes when I heard the news:
    News of strange and evil doings here. Women are leaving home
    to follow Bacchus, they say, to honor him in sacred rites.
    Our women run wild upon the wooded hills, dancing
    to honor this new God, Bacchus, whoever *he* is.
    They revel around the brimming bowl of wine
    and one by one they steal away to some secret nook   220
    to fuck with "satyrs" as if they were Maenads giving it up
    as some sacred act—Believe me, their Aphrodite comes first,
    and not this Bacchus.
               But listen! I'll put a stop to it!
    I've captured a few and thrown them into prison;
    and those who are still at large I'll hunt down
    on the mountain: that woman Ino, and my mother, Agave,
    who bore me to Echion, and Actaeon's mother, Autonoë—
    I'll shackle them all in irons, you'll soon see,
    and there will be an end to this Bacchic mischief.

    They tell me some stranger came from Lydia,   230
    a sorcerer and magician with golden locks perfumed,
    and rosy-cheeked from wine, and the glow in his eyes
    that Aphrodite gives. This stranger, I hear, is with them
    day and night, teaching maidens the Bacchic mysteries.
    But let them once set foot inside these walls
    and see if I don't put an end to his thyrsus rattling,
    and the bouncing of his golden curls. For so help me
    I will cut his head loose from his torso.
               He says
    Dionysus is a God, does he? He says he was once
    sewn up in Zeus' thigh, does he? Dionysus is dead,   240
    he and his lying mother, struck down by lightning
    because she swore that Zeus had lain with her.
    The man who says otherwise insults our faith
    and is fit for a hanging.
               But look what a wonder
    we have here! Tiresias the prophet, all dressed up

in a dappled fawnskin, and my mother's father? Ha!
This is too funny! Thrashing around those Bacchic wands!
Grandfather, really! Hey, old men! Have you lost your minds!
Come now, shake off those ivy leaves. Put down the thyrsus,
Grandpa. You, Tiresias! Was it you who put him up to this?   250
Do you welcome this new God among our people? Do you really
need another deity to profit from your trade as a prophet,
to help you read signs of flying birds and leaping flames?
Now, if your gray hairs did not plead for you,
I'd have you thrown in jail along with the Bacchae
for your complicity in their wicked, disgusting rites.
I tell you, where the grape brings joy to women's feasting,
no good ever comes of it, the service becomes an orgy.

CHORUS

Such impiety! Have you no reverence,
you strange man, no reverence for the Gods   260
or for Cadmus, who sowed this earth with the seed of men?
O son of Echion, you disgrace your people and your birth.

TIRESIAS

When a wise man has something to say, his words
come quickly on the tongue. Now, young sir,
while your words flow as freely as a wise man's,
there's not a grain of sense in your field of speech.
And a bold man in the seat of power—a man
of swift speech lacking good sense—is a real hazard
to the whole community. I say the new God you're mocking
will grow so powerful in Hellas, my poor words   270
cannot begin to describe His magnitude.
                                        Young man,
two Beings men hold in highest reverence:
the Goddess Demeter—that is the Earth—call her
either name you like, she serves men solid food.
Then as her partner came this new God, the son
of Semele. He drew forth sweet liquid from the grapes,

oh, precious gift to men, the juice of the vine,
that drowns each mortal's sorrows. Sleep also
he brings, kind sleep, erasing the day's remorse—
there is no better cure for a man's troubles.   280
This is the God that pleases other Gods
when time comes for libation; through him mankind
entreats the gifts of Heaven. And this is the God
you're mocking because some say he was stitched up
in Zeus' thigh . . . Well, listen and learn the truth:
After Zeus rescued the boy from the lightning's blaze
and lifted him to Olympus, Hera wanted to cast him down
from Heaven. Zeus, with a God's wit, hatched this plot:
He broke off a piece of the ether that girdles the earth
and from it he molded a likeness of Dionysus.   290
This he gave Hera as hostage while the real child
he spirited off somewhere so safe and secret it might
as well have been Zeus' thigh, as someone said.
Years pass, and the truth gives way to myth,
and so the story got garbled.
                      But mark my words:
This God knows the prophet's power, never doubt it.
The Bacchic frenzy inspires prophecy. When the God
flows into a body in full force, he makes
the wild-eyed believer tell the future. Then too
he is known to take a part in Ares' affairs: 300
You know the moment of tingling panic before the battle
when men stand in ranks, before anyone touches a spear?
Their frenzy is sent to men from Dionysus.
Over the high cleft rocks of Delphi, torch in hand,
you'll see him leaping, exalted, waving his thyrsus,
hailed all over Greece.
                    Hear me out, Pentheus.
Never brag that you can rule men by force alone,
and don't mistake your lame opinions for real wisdom.
Welcome this God to your realm. Spill wine,
join the revels, crown your head with ivy.   310
Dionysus does not control our women's modesty in love;

let us consider whether this chastity we prize
is really suitable to a woman's nature. If so,
no need to worry: worthy maidens will not be drawn
to the God's orgies. Now listen to me, my boy:
It warms your heart when thousands crowd your gates,
doesn't it, when the name of Pentheus is praised
by the whole town? Just so the God loves to be praised.

Go ahead and laugh at us, Cadmus and me! We'll dress
our brows with ivy, we'll dance, gray as we are,   320
we'll join in the merry-making! Nothing you can say
will make me cross the Gods. You're just insane,
so sadly crazed no medicine can save you.

CHORUS

Your speech, old man, is worthy of Apollo.
Honoring the great Bromius, you show deep wisdom.

CADMUS

Now, my son, Tiresias has given you sound advice.
Be on our side. Don't test the bounds of lawful custom.
You go flying off where your wisdom is not wisdom.
If you doubt the God is a god then lie a little,
tell a white lie for our glory, admit that Semele   330
is mother of a God. It's an honor for all our race!
And never forget the gruesome fate Actaeon met—
How the flesh-ripping dogs he trained turned on the man
and tore him apart in a meadow because he bragged,
within earshot of the Goddess, how he was better
at hunting than Artemis. Come, now, my boy, lest
you meet a similar fate, let me crown your head
with ivy, come along with us and honor the God.

PENTHEUS

Hands off! Go on and play at being Bacchants,
but don't infect me with your foolishness.   340
Let me get my hands on the man who taught you to be fools,

and I'll teach him a lesson.
                              Officers! Go at once
to his augury seat where he watches his birds,
and wreck it with crowbars, turn it upside down;
steal his crowns and scatter them to the winds.
See if this doesn't wound him. You, and you—go down
into the streets and track down this androgynous stranger
who has given our women this new disease, and done
such violence to our marriage bonds. When you catch him
bring him here in chains. Death by stoning   350
will make a bitter end to his party here in Thebes.

TIRESIAS

Poor fool, you really don't know what you're saying.
I thought you were "touched" before, but you're really crazy!
Let's go, Cadmus. We'll pray in earnest for this savage.
We'll pray for the city, too, that the God not punish
the whole populace in vengeance. Come follow me now
with your ivy wand. We'll hold each other up,
old tottering wrecks; wouldn't it be a sorry sight,
two old men fallen by the roadside? Enough of that.
We have our duty to Bacchus, son of Zeus.
                              O Cadmus!   360
Pentheus may bring anguish beyond repentance to your house.
No prophecy in those words, just plain facts.
The fool talks and talks nothing but rank foolishness.

CHORUS

O Sanctity, Queen of the Gods,
grazing the earth with your golden wings,
have you heard what Pentheus says,
do you hear his proud blasphemy
against Bromius, son of Semele,
first of the Gods at their banquets,
in beauty peerless? His duty   370
to lead the dancers, blend

the flute music with laughter
when the grape liquor flows
at the feast of the Gods,
when the wine bowl sheds sleep upon men
who wear their chaplets of ivy.
To men who spend words foolishly
flouting the law, comes misery;
but a quiet life ruled by reason
is bedrock for a man's house.   380
Far away are the powers of Heaven
but they never stop watching us.
They see what men do. Wisdom
is far more than cleverness. The man
who ventures out of his depth
in thought, scants the present,
and life is too short for this.
Who would leave his body
to chase a shadow? Only madmen
and fools, in my opinion.   390

Oh, fly me away to Aphrodite's
isle, Cyprus, where potent Gods
of love comfort man's soul;
or carry me to Paphos, the rainless
land the strange river nourishes
through a hundred mouths.
Oh lead me, Bromius, guide of all
the Bacchants, to the sacred slopes
of beautiful Olympus,
where Pierian muses dwell.   400
There the Graces live, and sweet Desire,
where men's laws cannot hinder
the joyful Bacchants' revel.

Oh, how our God loves feasting,
how he loves Peace, the son of Zeus,
Peace bountiful, the Goddess

who nourishes our youth.
He has granted the pleasure of wine
to rich and poor alike,
drowning sorrow. But he hates   410
all who scorn this joyful life,
the blessed days, the nights of bliss.
True wisdom it is
to keep your heart and mind free
of those high thoughts of the proud
men who think immoderately.
Oh, give me the simpler faith
of simple hearts! Follow the crowd!
(Pentheus enters from the palace. A servant follows with attendants
bringing Dionysus in chains.)

SERVANT
    See, Pentheus, you did not send us out in vain.
    Here is the prey you wanted us to catch. The beast   420
    was gentle and obedient, he did not run or struggle.
    His cheek never paled, he never lost that rosy color.
    He smiled and let me bind him to be led.
    It was so easy, I was a little embarrassed.
    I said to him: "Stranger, it's not my idea
    to arrest you, I'm just following orders."
                                    Now.
    The Bacchae you've caught so far, and shackled and jailed,
    all of them have sprung loose and fled to the meadows.
    They're skipping and dancing and praising their Bromian God;
    their shackles fell from their feet as if by magic;   430
    doors swung wide although no hand ever touched them.
    I tell you, this man has brought plenty of wonders to Thebes.
    I caught him, as you ordered. The rest is up to you.

PENTHEUS
    Free his hands. We have him in our power now
    and I don't think he's clever enough to escape. Oh

look what a darling he is, the handsome stranger!
What woman in Thebes could resist you? That long hair
is made for love, not wrestling! Those thick curls
bouncing on your cheeks, so sexy! Such white skin!
How do you get that effect? No bolts of sunlight for you,   440
that's for sure; you hunt for love in the shade
that pampers your beauty's lure.

> Tell me, who are your people?

DIONYSUS

There's an easy question a plain man can answer.
Maybe you've heard of flowery Tmolus?

PENTHEUS

I know it, the range of hills around Sardis town.

DIONYSUS

I come from there, and I was born in Lydia.

PENTHEUS

And where did you get these rites you've brought to Hellas?

DIONYSUS

Dionysus initiated me. Zeus' son.

PENTHEUS

So Lydia has a Zeus who begets new Gods?

DIONYSUS

No, it's the same Zeus, who wedded Semele in Thebes.   450

PENTHEUS

Did the God seduce you by night or in broad daylight?

DIONYSUS

He looked me right in the eyes as he taught me the rites.

PENTHEUS

What rites? What orgies? Tell us! What mysteries?

DIONYSUS

That's a secret only known to initiates.

PENTHEUS

What do they get out of it, the initiates?

DIONYSUS

This is not for your ears—though it's worth knowing.

PENTHEUS

That's clever. You make me hunger to hear more.

DIONYSUS

But the orgies resist the man who defies God.

PENTHEUS

You saw this God. Can you tell me how he is made?

DIONYSUS

As suits a God; I had nothing to do with it.   460

PENTHEUS

Again you find clever ways of saying nothing.

DIONYSUS

Only a fool would waste wisdom on a fool.

PENTHEUS

Is this the first place you've come with your new God?

DIONYSUS

All the Barbarians dance to the drum of his orgies.

PENTHEUS
Because they are backward. Less wise than the Greeks.

DIONYSUS
Wiser in this, although their ways seem strange.

PENTHEUS
Do you perform these rites by day, or night?

DIONYSUS
By night, mostly. Darkness lends solemnity.

PENTHEUS
And women are snared more easily in the dark.

DIONYSUS
Daylight serves just as well the master of lust.   470

PENTHEUS
Enough! You'll pay for your crimes and insolence.

DIONYSUS
You'll pay double for your folly and disrespect.

PENTHEUS
What a fighter this Bacchant is, if words were swords!

DIONYSUS
What terrible fate have you planned for me?

PENTHEUS
Well, first I will cut off your pretty curls.

DIONYSUS
But my hair is sacred to the God!

PENTHEUS
Next, hand me the thyrsus. Hand it over!

DIONYSUS
Take it from me. This is Dionysus' wand!

PENTHEUS
Now we'll throw your carcass in the dungeon.

DIONYSUS
The God himself will free me when I'm ready.   480

PENTHEUS
Sure . . . when the Bacchae join you, calling his name . . .

DIONYSUS
He's near me now, he sees how I'm being treated.

PENTHEUS
Really, where? My eyes can't seem to find him.

DIONYSUS
Right here. You can't see him, you godless man.

PENTHEUS
Seize him! He's mocking me and all of Thebes.

DIONYSUS
Back, madmen! Don't be fools. Don't bind my hands.

PENTHEUS
I say, bind him, and I am in charge here.

DIONYSUS
You have nothing in your head, not a grain of wisdom.
You don't know what you're doing or who you are.

PENTHEUS
>I am Pentheus, son of Agave and Echion!   490

DIONYSUS
>You shall live up to your name, which rhymes with sadness.

PENTHEUS
>Out of my sight! Take him, shut him away
>in some horse's stall where he may smile at the darkness.
>Dance there, wretch. And as for those women
>who followed you and shared your depravities,
>I'll sell them as slaves or make them servants of my own;
>I'll chain them to looms far out of reach of your evil drums.

DIONYSUS
>I'll go. And I'll suffer no fate worse than Fate ordains.
>You mocked me. Dionysus will have his revenge.
>You say He doesn't exist. I say you're wrong.   500
>I feel his anguish now as you drag me off to prison.
>*(Dionysus exits.)*

CHORUS
>Dirce, sacred fountain,
>River Achelous' daughter, happy maiden,
>You bathed the boy in your waters
>after Zeus who begat him, saved him
>from a fire that would not die,
>and tucked him away in his thigh,
>crying "Come now, my wild little poem
>and enter your father's womb,
>for I will proclaim the God Bacchus   510
>throughout Thebes; you will be famous."
>Why then, blessed Dirce,
>do you turn me away when I come
>with garlands to celebrate here?
>You scorn me, fly from me. Why?

I swear by the vine of Bacchus,
the grace of his clustering grapes,
time will come you will turn to Bacchus.

No man born of the earth
can ever conceal his breeding.   520
Pentheus is a dragon's grandson.
Though the earth-born Echion
had a hand in his making, sired him,
he has the fierce looks of a Titan,
a murderous giant, not a man,
pitting himself against Heaven.
Now he will bind me, the handmaiden
of Bromius, now he will keep
my fellow revelers shut
within his walls, locked deep   530
in a gloomy crypt in his palace.

Do you see this, Dionysus?
Son of Zeus, do you see your prophets
straining against their chains?
Come, King, with your golden wand swinging
down the slope of Olympus, come
put this proud beast in his place.
Oh where are you, Dionysus?
Nysa, where wild beasts graze
On the peaks of Corycus is your thyrsus   540
rounding up revelers?
Maybe you are deep in the forest
on Olympus where Orpheus once
made the trees dance with his lyre
and summoned the beasts of the fields.
Oh blessed Pieria,
Dionysus loves this land.
He will come to lead the dance,
He will cross swift-flowing Axius

with Maenads circling round him.   550
He will cross the Lydian river
which brings joy and wealth to men,
cross the father of rivers
whose water we know blesses
land that breeds the best horses.

DIONYSUS *(from within)*

Yo! Do you hear me, ladies?
Yo, Bacchants, do you hear me now?

CHORUS (1)

Who cried out? Where did that voice come from? Evius?

DIONYSUS

Yo! I'll call out again, hear the son of Semele and Zeus!

CHORUS (2)

Hail master, our master, Yo!   560

CHORUS

Come down to our revel-band,
you, rhythm-King, Bromius!

DIONYSUS

Now, feel the earthquake under my dancing feet?
(Dionysus enters from the palace, dancing, but they do not see him.)

CHORUS (3)

Oh, feel it! The rafters of Pentheus' house
are shaking like sticks. Soon it will totter and fall.
Dionysus is in there! Bow down and show him respect!

CHORUS (4)

We worship him.
Look where the stone lintel
is cracked from the pillars trembling!
The house can't hold the war-cry of our rhythm-King!   570

DIONYSUS

Oh, light me a fiery-red torch from a lightning bolt.
Burn, burn the palace of Pentheus to the ground.

CHORUS (5)

Look at the flames!
See where the fire is lighting
the sacred tomb of Semele
where fire once came from Zeus' lightning bolts.

CHORUS (6)

Down on your knees, now
bow low to the ground, you Maenads;
here comes the son of Zeus, our King.
He will shake that palace to cinders.   580
(Part of the palace is destroyed. Dionysus enters from an
undamaged doorway.)

DIONYSUS

Barbarian women, are you so scared you cannot stand?
You saw how Bacchus rattled the roofbeams of Pentheus' house.
Lift your hearts ladies, lift your bodies, put fear aside!

CHORUS

O, guiding light of our happy Bacchic revels,
we are so glad you have come. We were lost without you.

DIONYSUS

Were you sad when they led me into that house
and buried me in the darkness of Pentheus' dungeon?

CHORUS (1)

How should I not be troubled?
Who would protect me if luck failed you?
How did you get away from that god-hating man?   590

DIONYSUS

Easily. I was my own salvation.

CHORUS

But didn't he bind your hands with heavy ropes?

DIONYSUS

I tricked him there. While he thought he was tying me,
it was all an illusion I made. He never touched me.
In the stables where he meant to imprison me, he mistook
a bull for my body, bound up his legs, huffing and puffing
in fury, gnashing his teeth, and sweating while I sat nearby
enjoying the show.
                Then came the power of Bacchus making
the house quake, lighting the fire again at his mother's tomb.
But Pentheus thought his palace was burning down,   600
and ran up and down in a panic screaming at servants,
"Fire, bring water!" But all their work was in vain.
So he paused long enough to remember I might have escaped,
stormed into the palace, unsheathing his murderous sword.
Then Bromius, I believe (I can only tell you what I saw),
set loose a phantom of himself in those halls.
Pentheus pursued it, stabbing the bright air,
thinking he'd murder me.
              Bacchus still wasn't done
tormenting the man. He dashed his house to the ground
and smashed it to pieces. There it lies in ruins,   610
a bitter reminder how shamefully he served me.
At last he was too tired to hold up his sword
and fell into a faint. So does the mortal fare
who fights a God. Meanwhile I was long gone,
out of that house to be with you here. Who cares
about Pentheus? But I suspect we'll see him soon.
I hear footsteps. I wonder what he will say,
after all that's happened? Well let him rage.
I'll be calm. A wise man never loses his temper.

PENTHEUS *(entering)*
> Outrageous insults! The stranger I jailed   620
> has escaped! Ha! There's the man. What's this?
> How can you be walking out here when you're chained in there?

DIONYSUS
> Easy, fellow. Tread softly in your anger.

PENTHEUS
> But you were chained! How is it you're free now?

DIONYSUS
> Didn't you hear me say someone would free me?

PENTHEUS
> Who? You have said so many peculiar things.

DIONYSUS
> The One whose gift to men is the clustered vine.

PENTHEUS
> [The One whose gift to women is lewd nights?]

DIONYSUS
> Now, there's a sly joke at the God's expense.

PENTHEUS
> Officers, man the towers all around!   630

DIONYSUS
> What for? You think your walls can halt the Gods?

PENTHEUS
> Oh you're wise, wise except for what you ought to know.

DIONYSUS

What most concerns me—in this I am wise enough.
But don't listen to me, here comes a messenger. Listen
to him, for he comes from the hills with news for you.
(A messenger, a cowherd, enters.)
I'll wait here. You needn't fear I'll run away.

MESSENGER

Pentheus, Lord of Thebes: I come from Cithaeron,
where snowflakes shine the whole year through—

PENTHEUS

Yes, yes, and what is your precious news?

MESSENGER

I have seen the Bacchae, the inspired ones   640
who left this land in a frenzy, their white feet flying.
And I am here to tell you and your citizens what marvels,
what awesome scenes they are enacting. Should I speak freely
of these things? Perhaps I should avoid certain details
you might find unpleasant . . . in truth, my Lord,
I am afraid of your quick temper, your royal fury.

PENTHEUS

Speak. You shall be blameless in my eyes.
An honest man must never be met with fury.
But the worse you speak of the Bacchae,
the worse will be our sentence upon the man   650
who has taught our women his abominable arts.

MESSENGER

Well, I was just driving my cattle to the ridge.
The sun had sent forth its rays to warm the earth.
I came upon three bands of dancing women,
one led by Autonoë, and one by your mother, Agave;
Ino led the third company. They were rising from sleep

and stretching sweetly; here and there some lolled
on pine-branch pallets, others rested their heads
on pillows of oak-leaves.
                              The women seemed modest,
not as you say, dancing lewdly to flutes or drunk on wine,   660
or hunting for sex on lonely paths in the forest.
But then your mother stood up in their midst
and shouted for the Bacchae to wake up, for she'd heard
the sound of my horned cattle. And then those women,
a wonder of beauty to behold, sat bolt upright,
rubbing the sleep from their eyes, all refreshed,
the young women and the old, and unwed maidens. First
they let down their hair to grace their shoulders,
and fastened fawnskins tight if they'd come undone,
clasping their dresses while adoring snakes   670
licked their necks and cheeks. Some took in their arms
suckling kids or wolves' whelps, nursing these,
mothers who'd left their infants, whose full breasts
ached to feed their pure milk to the strange beasts.
They put on crowns of ivy, oak, wreaths of star-flowers.
One took her thyrsus, struck it on a rock, and there
gushed a spring of purest water, another stuck
her wand in the earth's lap, whence the God sent up
a spring of wine. Any who had the craving for white milk,
had only to scratch the ground with fingertips   680
to sluice all they could drink.
                              My Lord, had you been there
and seen such things, you would have dropped to your knees
and praised the God you now blame for everything.

We met in council, herdsmen and shepherds together
to ponder all of these strange and fearful wonders.
And one fellow, a sort of street-corner orator,
stood up among us and shouted "You men who live
on the sacred mountain terraces! I say
we hunt down Agave, Pentheus' mother,

bring her back from the Bacchic revels.   690
He'll consider this a kind service to the State."
We liked his speech.
                    So we hid in ambush in a thicket.
And when time came for them to whirl the thyrsus
in their Bacchic rite, calling in one voice
on Iacchus, the Bromian God, the son of Zeus,
the mountainside rang with their cries, every bird and beast,
the ground of nature trembled as they rushed by.
Now, suddenly, by chance, who should come bounding
past me, but Agave. Hoping to grab her,
I left my place in hiding, a rash move. For then   700
she shouted out: "Come now, my fleetfooted hounds!
These men are hunting us! Come follow me, come running,
armed with the thyrsus." They turned upon us. We fled
and just escaped the ravening clutches of the Bacchants.

They attacked our grazing cattle with their bare hands,
more terrible than swords. I saw one woman
tear into a bull calf that bellowed piteously,
and others ripping heifers to pieces with nails and teeth.
Here you would see bloody ribs scattered,
and there hooves hurled far away. Bits of flesh   710
hung, dripping blood from the pine branches.
Before our fierce bulls could lower heads to charge,
countless maiden hands had conquered them
and wrestled them to the ground. Before you could wink
your royal eye, my Lord, those virgins had skinned
those bulls alive!
                    Then they took off like birds
in flight for the plain along the stream Asopus
whose richness makes your bountiful Theban harvest.
They swooped down on the towns of Hysiae and Erythrae
which lie beneath the crags of Cithaeron,   720
wreaking havoc, turning everything upside down.
They dragged children from their homes, took
whatever they pleased, hoisting on their bare shoulders

heavy brass and iron loot which somehow balanced
without cords, Oh, wondrous! They dropped not a stick
on the dark earth. Then, wonder of wonders, some townsmen
tried to torch their tresses: the hair wouldn't burn!
Men took up arms, enraged at the Bacchants' marauding.
Then we saw the most awesome spectacle: their spears
could not draw a drop of blood from the women,   730
while these hurled their thyrsi wounding the men
who turned their backs in flight, terrified.
Women routing the men, with the help of their God!
This done, they returned to where they had started,
back to the springs God had made to flow for them,
and washed their hands. Snakes slithered forth to lick
their necks and cheeks clean of every trace of gore.

My Lord, I beg you, receive this God, whoever he is,
into your city. After all I have said of his power,
there's more to say: I hear it is he that gave to men   740
the fruit of the vine which is Grief's nemesis.
Where there is no wine, Aphrodite will not come,
nor shall we know any other human pleasure.

CHORUS
Although I'm afraid to speak freely
before a tyrant, I must say what's on my mind:
There can be no God greater than Dionysus.

PENTHEUS
Like wildfire the Bacchae's audacity
is spreading! What an embarrassment to the Greeks.
No time to spare. You, go to the Electran gate.
Command the shield-bearing soldiers to gather here   750
with horsemen who bridle their swift-footed steeds;
summon the archers who make the bowstrings hum,
and we will launch an attack against the Bacchae.
We have had more than we can take from these women.
(The messenger exits.)

DIONYSUS

Oh, Pentheus! Have you learned nothing after all
you've heard? As much as I've suffered at your hands,
still I'll counsel you: Never take arms against a God.
Go easy. I'm telling you this for your own good.
Bromius will not endure it. He won't stand by
while you drive his Bacchants from their haunts in the hills.   760

PENTHEUS

You dare lecture me? Count yourself fortunate
you've escaped the dungeon. Be still or I'll jail you again.

DIONYSUS

If I were you I would offer Him sacrifice. Don't
knock your poor skull against rock, a mere man against God.

PENTHEUS

I'll offer a sacrifice: a broad slaughter of females.
How's that? Dead women shall fill the glen of Cithaeron.

DIONYSUS

No. They'll put you to shame. The Bacchae's wands
will scatter your warriors with their shields of bronze.

PENTHEUS

Listen to him! Will he never stop making trouble?
Whether free or tied, the stranger runs his mouth.   770

DIONYSUS

My friend, there is still time to save the day.

PENTHEUS

How? Shall I become the slave of my slaves?

DIONYSUS

Look, I will bring the women here unarmed.

PENTHEUS
  Ha! This must be some sort of trick.

DIONYSUS
  By my trickery I intend to save you.

PENTHEUS
  You've plotted with the Bacchae to save your revels.

DIONYSUS
  No, but I have an agreement with the God.

PENTHEUS
  Bring me my sword. You, give your tongue a rest.

DIONYSUS
  Wait! Would you like to see them sitting on the hillside?

PENTHEUS
  I would indeed. A load of gold no man could measure   780
  I would give to see them.

DIONYSUS
  Why this sudden change of heart?

PENTHEUS
  I would like to see them helplessly drunk.

DIONYSUS
  Would it please you, to see that sorry sight?

PENTHEUS
  Yes, if I could watch quietly through the pines.

DIONYSUS
  But they will attack you if they see you skulking.

PENTHEUS
> You're right. I'll be bold and stand in the open.

DIONYSUS
> So. Shall I be your guide? Are you ready to go?

PENTHEUS
> Right now. Lead on. Don't waste any precious time!

DIONYSUS
> First, you must put on these linen robes.   790

PENTHEUS
> What? I'm a man! Do you take me for a woman?

DIONYSUS
> If they see you are a man, they will murder you.

PENTHEUS
> Wise words. I never said you weren't clever.

DIONYSUS
> Dionysus taught me all these things.

PENTHEUS
> How shall I best go about this business?

DIONYSUS
> Come into the house, my friend. I will dress you.

PENTHEUS
> In that lady's gown? No, I'd be ashamed!

DIONYSUS
> Then I guess you don't really want to see the Maenads.

PENTHEUS
Well. How, exactly, would you have me look?

DIONYSUS
First I would like your hair long and curly.   800

PENTHEUS
Then?

DIONYSUS
A floor-length skirt. A turban on your head.

PENTHEUS
Anything else?

DIONYSUS
A thyrsus to hold, a fawnskin wrap.

PENTHEUS
But . . . but I can't wear a woman's clothes.

DIONYSUS
Then fight the Bacchae and dress yourself in blood.

PENTHEUS
I see your reasoning. First, I'll spy on them.

DIONYSUS
It's better sport than hunting evil by evil paths.

PENTHEUS
But how can I pass through Cadmus' streets unnoticed?

DIONYSUS
I'll guide you along deserted roads. Come, now.   810

PENTHEUS

It would be just awful, to hear the Bacchae mock me.

DIONYSUS

Come inside, we'll see that everything's done right.

PENTHEUS

I'll go. If I'm not going to wear my sword,
I may as well wear what you think will suit the occasion.
(Pentheus enters that part of the palace that still stands.)

DIONYSUS

Ladies! Our man walked right into the trap!
He'll visit the Bacchae and pay the penalty of death.
O Dionysus, now is the time for you to take over.
You are not far away. Let's take our revenge:
First, drive him out of his mind, fill his brain with frenzy.
If he's sane he'll never wear a woman's dress, but   820
once he's gone off his head he'll put on anything. Oh!
How I look forward to making him a laughingstock in Thebes,
leading him through the streets in a woman's getup,
after all his menacing threats! Now it's time to dress
Pentheus in clothes he must wear to Hades
after he dies by his mother's hand. He shall know
Dionysus, son of Zeus, the God who truly is
the kindest and the cruelest of all to mankind.

CHORUS

Now I shall dance all night,
my feet flashing quick and white   830
in honor of Dionysus, my neck bare,
feeling Heaven's dewy air.
Now I shall leap like a fawn
on the joyful green of the lawn,
just after she's slipped the noose,
the woven nets, running loose
and fleet along the plain,

leaping the river, free of man,
hearing the hunter and hounds cry
far away. She exults in the shade   840
of a solitary glade.

What gift of Gods to men
is more lovely than wisdom
or the glory of mastery
over a fallen enemy?
Such glory endures forever.

Never fear. The God will chide
fools who, in their pride
begrudge honor to Heaven's king
by grave faults in their reasoning.   850
Gods know how to hide
and hunt down the infidel.
No man can match God's stride
through the years. Don't override
the tried customs, the old ways.
It costs him little who says:
As God's power must ever endure,
likewise our long-standing laws
show the will of Divine Nature.

What gift of Gods to men   860
is more lovely than wisdom
or the glory of mastery
over a fallen enemy?
Such glory endures forever.

He's a happy man who escapes
sea-wrack, reaches the harbor;
he's happy who's done
with hard labor. One
piles up a fortune, another
rises to power—the shapes   870

hope takes are different for each man.
Some dreams end in happiness,
some sadly fade away.
The happiest man never reaches
for bliss, but takes joy
as he finds it, yes,
takes his joy day by day.

DIONYSUS *(calling within)*

Now, my eager spy! You, so impatient to be a part
of all you so lately scorned, you, Pentheus!
Come out of the house now, let's have a look at you,   880
all dressed up like a woman, a frenzied Bacchant,
all ready to spy on your mother and her band!
*(Pentheus enters dressed like a woman, in fawnskin and wearing a wig
and make-up.)*
How sweet! You do look just like one of Cadmus' daughters!

PENTHEUS

My, oh my! I think I see two suns up there,
and two towns of Thebes, our seven-gated city!
And you, my guide? I believe you must be a bull,
because I can see the horns sprouting on your head.
Were you ever an animal? I swear you look like a bull!

DIONYSUS

Then the God is with us! He graces our presence
at last, an ally. You're seeing just as you should see.   890

PENTHEUS

Tell me, truthfully, how do I look? Don't I remind you
a little of Ino, or of my mother Agave, in this pose?

DIONYSUS

The very spit and image! But here, darling,
this curl is out of place, let me tuck it back
under the turban, the way I had it before . . .

PENTHEUS

Oh, dear, I must have shaken it loose back there
when I was dancing up and down in Bacchic frenzy.

DIONYSUS

Don't fret. I'll smooth it out. After all,
it's my pleasure to be your . . . beautician. But stand still!

PENTHEUS

Be sure to get it right. I'm counting on you.   900

DIONYSUS

Now your girdle is loose! And your skirt!
I don't like how it hangs crooked below your ankles.

PENTHEUS

Let's see . . . I agree with you about the right side,
but as for the left—ooh, I just love the way the robe
clings to the curve of my thigh . . .

DIONYSUS

You won't forget old friends like me, I hope
after the Bacchae have dazzled you with their virtues.

PENTHEUS

But how do I hold the thyrsus to look most
like a Bacchant? In the right hand, or the left?

DIONYSUS

Hold it in your right hand, and step out   910
with the right foot, so. Oh, I like your new attitude!

PENTHEUS

Am I man enough to carry them on my shoulders—
the Bacchants and Cithaeron glen? Am I ready for that?

DIONYSUS

Whatever you want. For a long time, your mind
was shaky, but now you are just as you need to be.

PENTHEUS

Levers? Should I use levers or my bare hands
to uproot the landscape, working my shoulders under the crags?

DIONYSUS

No, silly! You mustn't damage the nymph's shrines
or upset the sanctum of Pan, where he plays his pipes.

PENTHEUS

Well said. Better not use brute force against women.   920
I'll hide in the pines where none can see or hear me.

DIONYSUS

Hide! Yes, hide where you must be hidden,
sly dog, to peep and spy at the Bacchanals.

PENTHEUS

Why I bet they're already tangled in the weeds,
in the throes of wild sex, as naked as jaybirds!

DIONYSUS

Get going now, you might catch them in the act—
that is, if the Bacchants don't catch you first.

PENTHEUS

Lead me right down the main thoroughfare of Thebes
for all to see—the one man brave enough to *act*!

DIONYSUS

Your nation's burden falls to you alone,   930
fearless hero. A great struggle lies ahead.
Now follow me. I will deliver you safely there.
Someone else will bring you home.

PENTHEUS
>She who made me.

DIONYSUS
>You will be an example to all men.

PENTHEUS
>This is my mission, my destiny!

DIONYSUS
>And you will be carried home shoulder-high—

PENTHEUS
>Such a fuss!

DIONYSUS
>In your mother's arms

PENTHEUS
>Well, if you insist—   940

DIONYSUS
>Just a little pampering—

PENTHEUS
>I suppose I *do* deserve it, after all.
>*(Pentheus exits.)*

DIONYSUS
>Awful man. Shocking! But he will come to an end
>so terrible his pain will make him famous in Heaven.
>Reach out your hands to him, Agave, and you too,
>sisters, daughters of Cadmus. I'm leading this man
>to a battle royal which Dionysus and I will win
>handily. In a moment you'll see how it turns out.

CHORUS

Run to the mountains, you dogs
of madness, run swiftly now   950
to the place where the daughters of Cadmus
hold their revels. Stir these women
into a frenzy against the man
tricked out in a woman's dress,
this man who spies on the Maenads.

First his mother shall see him
behind a slick rock or through
a forked tree. And she
will call to the Maenads:
"Who is this Cadmean who   960
comes to the mountain of mountains
to spy on us, O Bacchae?
Whose child could this be?
Not born of a woman's blood,
but some lioness maybe
or Libyan gorgon made him."

Now let Justice step up,
let her come with her sword drawn
and drive it straight through the throat
of this monstrous child of the earth,   970
this godless, lawless man,
the offspring of Echion.
With his filthy thoughts and lawless spite
against your mysteries, Bacchus,
and your mother's sacred rite,
he plots. This frail man
with sick thoughts and wild ideas,
somehow still believes he can
overcome your divine might.

He who would guard life from grief   980
knows God's wisdom is not meant for man;

he must never presume upon Heaven.
I envy no man his wisdom,
no matter how subtle or deep.
The greatest joy shall come
of truth known in eternity:
A man should live each day
in holiness and purity,
within the pale of custom
pursuing some noble goal,   990
and honoring Gods in humility.

Now let Justice step up,
let her come with her sword drawn
and drive it straight through the throat
of this monstrous child of the earth,
this godless, lawless man,
the offspring of Echion.

Come to us now, Bacchus!
Appear as a bull or dragon
with a hundred heads, or as   1000
a fire-breathing lion.
O Bacchus, come!
And with a wry grin
cast a noose around this hunter
tracking the Bacchanal, just when
He swoops down upon the Maenads.
(A messenger from Cithaeron enters.)

MESSENGER

    O house, all of Greece reveres you, that prospered so
                many years!
    House of the old Sidonian prince, who sowed the dragon's seed
    that yielded men, Oh house! I may be a slave but still I weep
                for you.
    A good servant can share his master's sadness   1010
    when such a disaster as this has come to pass.

CHORUS
What is it? Can you give us news of the Bacchae?

MESSENGER
Echion's son, Pentheus, is dead.

CHORUS
O Bromius, my King! You are a great God, and now you
prove it!

MESSENGER
How can you talk like that at such a time?
Are you celebrating your master's doom?

CHORUS
I'll shout my joy like any Barbarian! Once I was bound here
like an alien slave. Now I'm free of my chains!

MESSENGER
Weigh your words. There are still men in Thebes.

CHORUS
O Dionysus, Dionysus is my Lord, not Thebes.   1020

MESSENGER
Then you might be forgiven; but beware—
It's not right to enjoy such a catastrophe.

CHORUS
But tell me, tell me his fate!
How did he die, this lawless wretch?

MESSENGER
We had set out from Therapnae here in Thebes,
and crossing the stream of Asopus we'd started to mount
the heights of Cithaeron, Pentheus and I. For I

went with them, my master and the stranger who was
to guide us the scene.
                    We paused to sit awhile
in a grassy valley, not daring to breathe or let our steps   1030
be heard, for we wished to see without being seen.
There was a little glen watered by creeks,
walled in by rocks and shaded by the pines;
and in that glen we saw the Maenads sitting,
their hands at joyful work. Some were making
fresh ivy crowns for the frayed thyrsus; others,
like horses glad to be free from painted yokes,
frolicked, singing the hymns of Bacchic rapture.
Then Pentheus, poor wretch, not seeing the crowd of women,
cried out:
                    "Stranger, I can't quite see the Maenads   1040
from where I stand. What do you say, I'll climb
on that mound, or a high pine? Then I'll have
a better view of the Maenads' lewd carousing."
Then I saw the stranger work a wonder:
reaching a high pine bough by its very tip
he pulled it earthward, lower and lower still,
till it bent like a bow or a lathe-turned wheel
that comes full circle—just so the stranger pulled
that mountain pine to the ground with immortal strength.
Then he seated Pentheus in its limbs, with gentle hands,   1050
so he would not tumble from his perch as the tree sprung
straight skyward, holding up my master enthroned
for all the Maenads to see! Oh, he never saw them
as they beheld him! For no sooner did they see
him riding high, than the stranger vanished and
a voice came from the sky—it must have been Dionysus—
speaking these words:
                    "Maidens, I give you the man
who made you and me and all our sacred rites
a laughing stock. Now take your vengeance upon him."
As he spoke he cast from Heaven to earth   1060
a dazzling shaft of flame. The sky was hushed.

Not a leaf in the green valley rustled, not a creature
made a sound, though all who heard that voice
stood upright and looked nervously all around.
Once again he commanded them.

        And when Cadmus' daughters
were certain this was Bacchus, these were his orders,
they came running swift as doves and eager to please.
His mother Agave, her sisters, and all the Bacchae
came bounding over the rocks and rapids of the valley.
And when they came to my master perched in the pine,   1070
first they threw stones at him with all their might
from a high rock nearby. Some threw pine branches,
others launched their thyrsi through the air
at Pentheus, their doomed target, but they missed.
He was treed but just out of their eager reach,
the poor wretch; there he sat, helpless, hopeless,
panicked.

    At last they cracked oak limbs with a noise
like thunder, intending to use these as levers
to pry the mountain fir loose from the soil.
When this would not do the job, Agave said   1080
"Come gather around the tree trunk, Maenads,
get a good grip. If we don't catch the beast
who is roosting there he will betray the secrets
of our God's dancing-place." A myriad hands
seized the pine-trunk, wrenched it from the ground.
And Pentheus, from his great height, crashed to earth,
screaming and crying. He knew he was done for.
First his mother descended on him, as a priestess.
She started the bloody business. And he, thinking that she
might recognize him, stripped the turban from his hair,   1090
hoping she would not kill him. He stroked her cheek,
pleading:

    "Mother, it is your own child, Pentheus,
the boy you bore in Echion's house. Have mercy, Mother!
Do not murder me for a few transgressions."

But Bacchus possessed her. Foaming at the mouth
and rolling her eyes around, she did not heed him.
Out of her mind, she seized his left hand in her grip,
and, standing on his chest, she ripped off his arm
from the socket, not by her own strength but by the God's.
Then Ino got to work on the other arm, tearing it loose   1100
while Autonoë and the rest of the crowd of Bacchants
joined in, and their war cries and the victim's rasping
groans were as one chorus. One girl ripped a hand away,
another prized a severed foot still in its sandal.
Ribs they stripped clean of flesh with their rending nails;
bloody hands played catch with Pentheus' limbs.

Now his corpse lies scattered all around: a piece here
under a rugged stone, and there, deep in the forest shade.
Gathering it together will be no easy task.
As for his poor head, his mother has taken this   1110
into her own hands, and stuck it on top of her thyrsus.
She holds the bloody head high in pride as if
she had slain a mountain lion. She leaves her sisters
dancing with Maenads while she strides through Cithaeron
bearing that trophy head aloft in jubilation.
The walls resound with her joy as she calls on Bacchus
her fellow huntsman who helped her triumph in the chase.
But she has won a bitter victory whose prize is tears.

Now let your faithful servant depart in peace,
away from this pitiful scene, before Agave gets home.   1120
Oh, humble wisdom and reverence for the Gods
outshine any other prize a mortal can gain.
The man is wisest who owns these, in my opinion.

CHORUS
Now let us praise Bacchus,
dancing and singing in chorus
the fall of Pentheus, the dragon's heir

who dressed up like a woman,
took up the thyrsus fair
and with a bull for his guide,
met with fierce calamities,   1130
bearing his wand to Hades.
O Bacchants, Cadmean maidens,
victory now is yours;
but your victory song
shall end in heartache and tears.
Oh, what a great triumph of motherhood:
the mother's hands steeped in the hot blood
of her son, till her fingers drip with it.
(Agave enters bearing the head of Pentheus stuck on her thyrsus.)
But look, here comes Agave now,
the mother of Pentheus,   1140
her eyes starting out of her head.
Welcome, reveler! Praise the Evian God!

AGAVE
Bacchants of Asia!

CHORUS
Yes. You call to us?

AGAVE
I have come down from the mountain
with this young sprig of ivy to deck the halls.

CHORUS
We have eyes. Welcome to our revels.

AGAVE
I caught him without a snare,
a young lion. Come, have a look at him.

CHORUS
Where was he? The desert?   1150

AGAVE
Cithaeron.

CHORUS
Cithaeron?

AGAVE
We killed him there.

CHORUS
Who struck him first?

AGAVE
I had the privilege. Oh, lucky Agave,
they call me in our revel-band!

CHORUS
And who struck him then?

AGAVE
Cadmus—

CHORUS
But how could Cadmus—

AGAVE
His daughters attacked the monster after I did.   1160

CHORUS
You are a lucky woman, lucky indeed!

AGAVE
Come now and share the feast.

CHORUS
But . . . what part of this feast could I enjoy?

AGAVE

>Here—the flesh is tender under the chin
>where the down is scarcely grown; look at his curls!

CHORUS

>It is something like the hair of a wild beast.

AGAVE

>Oh, how that skillful hunter, the Bacchic God
>led his Maenads against this savage, so artfully!

CHORUS

>Oh, yes, our King is a great hunter.

AGAVE

>And you applaud me?   1170

CHORUS

>I praise you to the skies!

AGAVE

>Soon the whole race of Cadmus—

CHORUS

>Even Pentheus your son?

AGAVE

>He'll praise his mother for hunting this lion down.

CHORUS

>Strange game.

AGAVE

>And strangely caught.

CHORUS

>Are you happy now?

AGAVE

    I am in my glory. For I have done a great thing
    for my country; and now the world can see it!

CHORUS

    Show us, now, show all of us the prize   1180
    of victory you've brought us, you poor woman.

AGAVE

    Come one and all who live within the walls,
    these beautiful, tall-towered walls of Thebes.
    Draw near me now in my moment of glory so you can see
    the wild beast we've captured, the daughters of Cadmus and I.
    We hunted him down, not with Thessalian javelins
    launched from afar, not with snares, but with our bare hands,
    our lily-white arms and delicate fingers. Let men brag
    about fine weapons of skilled armorers, that rust away.
    With bare hands we women have dragged down our prey   1190
    and torn this vicious monster limb from limb.

    Father? Where is the old man? I want him to come.
    And where is my son, Pentheus? Tell him to come
    bring us a ladder, raise it against the house
    and nail his head to a beam, the lion I hunted down.
(Cadmus enters leading attendants carrying the dismembered body of
Pentheus on a bier.)

CADMUS

    Follow me now, my servants, up to the house,
    and bring along the sad burden of Pentheus.
    After endless searching we gathered his body together;
    it was strewn from one end of Cithaeron to the other
    all over the valley, scattered in thickets and weeds.   1200
    Someone informed me of my daughter's daring deeds,
    the minute I set foot within the city's walls

with old Tiresias, as we came home from the Bacchanal.
I turned back to the hills to bring home my grandson
who was killed by the Maenads. There I saw Autonoë,
she who bore Actaeon himself to Aristaeus, she and Ino
were wandering the grove, still crazed, the poor creatures.
But one told me Agave was on her way here, racing
as if Bacchus himself was making her feet fly.
This wasn't a lie. I see her myself. What a sorry sight!   1210

AGAVE

Father, blow your horn, brag all you please,
for no mortal man ever had such excellent daughters,
each and every one of them I mean, but not the least—
myself.
           I quit my shuttle at the loom
for a higher calling, the hunting of wild beasts
with my bare hands. I brought the prize home
in my arms so we might hang it there
on your palace wall.
                         Look, Father! Isn't it glorious?
Oh, I know you are proud of my hunting, so please
accept this, and summon all your friends to a feast   1220
in honor of our triumph. Oh, you are twice blessed!

CADMUS

I have only a man's eyes. How can I look
upon such infinite sorrow? Murder, hideous slaughter,
at your hands!
                    Oh, this is a handsome victim you offer
to the Gods! Then you call me and all of Thebes
to a feast of triumph? All I can do now is weep—
first for your boundless sorrows, then for mine.
Oh, how the God, the Bromian King, has worked our ruin;
this may be justice, but it's far too cruel.
And to think, we are his blood, his family!   1230

AGAVE

Listen to him! Old age does turn a man sour.
I would be thrilled if my son would take up hunting,
and if he might have as much luck as his mother
when he goes to chase savages with the boys of Thebes.
But all he seems fit to do is fight with the Gods.
You know we ought to warn him, father, you and I.
Where is he? Will somebody please call my son?
I want him here where I can see him and he can see
his mother in her finest hour. Oh, I am so happy!

CADMUS

You poor, deluded woman. When you wake up   1240
from this dream and realize what you have done,
you may wish you could live out all your days
in the cool shade of madness. You would not be truly happy
then either, but you would not be so cursed with grief . . .

AGAVE

What's this? What is the trouble? What grief?

CADMUS

First, my dear, look up. Look at the sky.

AGAVE

Well? What is it you want me to see there?

CADMUS

Is it the same as ever? Or do you think it changed?

AGAVE

Well, I think it's brighter . . . and clearer now . . .

CADMUS

Do you still feel that turbulence in your soul?   1250

AGAVE

    I'm not sure . . . what you just said . . . but wait . . .
    I think my mind is clearing like the sky. I'm coming around . . .

CADMUS

    Now can you hear my voice, and answer clearly?

AGAVE

    Oh, Father! I've forgotten all I said before!

CADMUS

    Whose house did you enter as a bride?

AGAVE

    You gave me to Echion, born of the dragon seed.

CADMUS

    And the son you bore your husband in that house—
    What was the boy's name?

AGAVE

                        Pentheus, our baby.

CADMUS

    And whose head is that in your arms?

AGAVE

    A lion's. At least that's what the hunters said.   1260

CADMUS

    Look closely now. It's not so hard to see—

AGAVE

    Ai! What's this? What are my hands holding?

CADMUS

    Look at it, now. Look! Until you are certain.

AGAVE

I see my grief—the worst vision of woe.

CADMUS

Now does it look like a lion?

AGAVE

No, no, it's Pentheus, his head I am holding!

CADMUS

Yes, We mourned him long before you knew.

AGAVE

How did he fall into my hands? Who killed my son?

CADMUS

Oh, the truth is so piteous, and comes too late.

AGAVE

Tell me! My heart will burst if I don't hear.   1270

CADMUS

You, you killed him. You and your sisters.

AGAVE

But . . . where? Where did he die? In the house? Where?

CADMUS

The same place where the dogs tore Actaeon apart.

AGAVE

But, my poor child! Why did he go there, to Cithaeron?

CADMUS

To make fun of the God, and your Bacchic rites.

AGAVE

And what were we doing, way up there?

CADMUS

You were out of your wits. Bacchus drove the whole city mad.

AGAVE

Dionysus drove us to ruin. I see it all, now.

CADMUS

The God was insulted. You denied he was truly a God.

AGAVE

Father, where is the body of my son?   1280

CADMUS

I gathered it piece by piece from the countryside.

AGAVE

Were you able to put him together at all?

CADMUS

[It's a sad sight, with or without this bloody head.]

AGAVE

What did my son's folly have to do with mine?

CADMUS

Like you, Pentheus denied homage to the God,
who then took his revenge, dragging you both down
to one ruin, destroying this once-noble house
and me, the last man to carry on the name.
Now I look at this boy, the fruit of your womb,
poor woman, I look at this child so shamefully slain.   1290
My child! My daughter's son! The hopes of our house
rested upon you, the city looked on you with awe.

As long as you lived no one would ever dare
show this old man any disrespect for fear
of quick reprisal. I've lost my young guardian.
Now I, the great Cadmus who saved the people of Thebes
and reaped such a rich harvest, I will be cast out
of my home, dishonored.

                Oh, my dear child!
Even in death you shall be counted dear to me
as any of my children. Though I shall never feel   1300
your hand on my cheek, or hear your voice again
calling me, your mother's sire, eager to know
"What's troubling you, old man? Who dares
to do you wrong, dishonor or vex your heart?
Tell me. I'll make him pay for it, Grandfather."

But now I am the saddest man on earth.
You are done for; your mother and sisters are ruined.
If there is anyone looking on who despises the Gods,
let him study this wreck of a man, and change his ways.

CHORUS

    I weep for you, Cadmus.   1310
    Although your daughter's child
    has met the fate he deserves,
    your grief is bitter, no less.

AGAVE

    O Father! Do you see how my life has changed!
    [A while ago I was strutting up and down
    with pride in my kill, triumphant. And now?
    I am tormented, burning with remorse. The prize
    I hurried to bring him is a curse upon us.
    These hands stained with my child's blood are accursed.
(She approaches the bier.)
    How can I touch his body with such hands?   1320
    How can I, a woman damned with such a deed,

take him in my arms, hold him to my breast?
O Gods, is there a death-song or lament
fit to lay each broken limb to rest?
This hand I held in mine when he was small
and took his first tottering steps. This foot
I kissed to make him laugh before he could talk.
Where is the other? Here! My heart must break
into as many pieces as lay jumbled here
of my poor son's life.   1330
                        Father, help me please,
put the boy together as he was? There, and there,
and gently lay his head, tilting it so. Oh sweet face!
Such a pretty mouth!
                        Hand me the shroud,
for even if these hands are cursed no other hands
shall wrap these bloody mangled limbs but mine,
his mother's. This is the flesh I brought to birth!

CHORUS
    Look at this scene, and learn God's lesson well.
(Dionysus appears on a raised platform.)

DIONYSUS
    Now hear me, men and women, heed the God.
    You scorned me, denying the homage I am due.
    Some slandered me, saying I came of mortal descent   1340
    and some who spoke blasphemy were not content
    but had to profane my person as well as my name.
    Long did I love them, care for them. And they
    in sheer malice repaid my kindness with vicious crimes.
    Now let it be known how they shall suffer:
    They shall be cast out of Thebes, to foreign lands,
    and there in slavery bound like prisoners of war,
    disgraced, they shall wear out their sorry lives.
(addressing the remains of Pentheus)
    This man found just the death that he deserved,
    torn apart and strewn among rough rocks.   1350

You saw it all: He came after me in a fury,
tried to chain and shut me in a dungeon;
he dared to abuse me by word and thought and deed.
And so, it is fitting he saw his executioners
were his own loved ones. His grim fate is fair.
As for you, Agave, and your sisters, this is your doom:
You too must leave this city to expiate
your violent crimes. You are so far defiled
it would be an outrageous sacrilege to find
such murderers living in sight of this burial ground.]   1360
Next, Cadmus: You shall be changed into a dragon,
you and your wife Harmonia as well,
Ares' child, who was yours in your mortal life,
shall shift from mortal to beast and back again
according to Zeus' oracle. You two shall drive
an ox-drawn chariot and lead the Barbarian
snake-tribes whose armies will plunder many towns
until they wreck the temple of Apollo. Then
they shall suffer grave misfortune returning home.
But be patient. Ares will rescue you and Harmonia   1370
and settle your lives in the Islands of the Blest.
How do I know these things? I am Dionysus,
son of Zeus, and not born of any mortal man.
If you had not kept turning away from wisdom,
you would be happy today, with Zeus on your side.

CADMUS
Dionysus, we have sinned. Forgive us, please!

DIONYSUS
Too late you recognized my power. Too late.

CADMUS
But now we know. You sentence is too severe.

DIONYSUS
I am a God, and you insulted me.

CADMUS

A God's wrath should not resemble the spite of men.   1380

DIONYSUS

Long ago my father Zeus ordained these things.

AGAVE

The die is cast, old man. We are poor exiles.

DIONYSUS

Why linger then, knowing the die is cast?

CADMUS

My child, what a terrible pass we have come to,
you, your poor sisters, and wretched me, at my age
forced to seek refuge in some foreign land
and abide there. But the oracle did declare
that I shall lead an army into Greece,
Barbarians whose spears I will command
in my dragon-shape. Ares' child, Harmonia,   1390
my wife and I as dragons will lead our troops
against the sacred shrines and tombs of Greece.
And trouble will go with me everywhere:
I shall find no peace even beyond Acheron.

AGAVE

O Father! I will lose you, you and my home!

CADMUS

What are you doing, poor girl? Do you think
your white arms will save me now with their embraces?
O my white swan, comforting her frail old sire.

AGAVE

Where will I go when I can't go home again?

CADMUS

    I don't know, child. Your father can't help you now.   1400

AGAVE

    Farewell, my home. Farewell, my native city.
    In sadness I leave you, an exile
    from the city and the home where I was wed.

CADMUS

    Go, my child, take refuge if you can
    in the house of Aristaeus.

AGAVE

    O Father, my heart aches for you.

CADMUS

    I weep for you, my dear. And for your sisters.

AGAVE

    Dionysus in his majesty brought down
    the cruelest vengeance on your noble house.

DIONYSUS

    And it was a cruel insult to my name   1410
    I suffered from you, who would not honor me in Thebes.

AGAVE

    Father, farewell.

CADMUS

    Farewell, my poor child. It's a hard road ahead.

AGAVE

    Take me now to where I can join my sisters.
    They shall be my companions in sorrowful exile.
    Let us go somewhere far out of sight of Cithaeron,

where it can't see me, and I can't see that cursed glen,
somewhere the memory of the thyrsus is not hallowed.
Let other Bacchants cherish those sacred things.

CHORUS

Divinity takes innumerable   1420
forms: the Gods surprise us as
what we planned for does not come to pass
while Heaven brings about the unthinkable.
All that has gone before is proof of this.

Pronouncing Glossary of Names

Stressed syllables are marked. The descriptions below are based primarily on the Oxford Classical Dictionary.

Achaeans (a-kee'-anz). Race of warlike bronze-age people who, with the Ionians, came into Greece from the north in the second millennium B.C. Achaea and Achaeans are often used as synonyms for Greece and the Greeks.

Achelous (a-kel'-oh-us). God of the river of the same name in Epirus.

Achilles (a-kil'-eez). Son of Peleus and Thetis, the best of the Greek warriors at Troy, and the hero of the *Iliad*.

Actaeon (ac-tay'-on). A famous huntsman who saw Artemis bathing, was changed into a stag, and was devoured by his own dogs.

Admetus (ad-meet'-us). King of Pherae and husband of Alcestis.

Adrastus (a-dras'-tus). One of the Seven against Thebes.

Aeacus (ee'-a-cus). King of the island of Oeopia, where, after a plague destroyed all his subjects, Zeus repopulated the kingdom by changing ants into humans.

Aegeus (ee-jee'-us). Son of Pandion and king of Athens. Father of Theseus by Aethra.

Aegisthus (ee-gis'-thus). Son of Thyestes, therefore a cousin of Agamemnon and Menelaus. Clytemnestra's lover.

Aegyptus (ee-jip'-tus). Son of Belus who gave his fifty sons in marriage to the fifty daughters of his brother Danaus. These brides murdered their grooms on their wedding night, all except Hypermnestra, who spared her husband Lynceus.

Agamemnon (ag-a-mem'-non). King of Mycenae, husband of Clytemnestra, and brother of Menelaus, king of Sparta. They were sons of Pleisthenes the son of Atreus (or, according to Homer, they were themselves sons of Atreus).

Agave (a-gav'-ay). Daughter of Cadmus, mother of Pentheus.

Agenor (ah-jee'-nor). King of Phoenicia, father of Cadmus.

Alcestis (al-ses'-tis). Wife of Admetus.

Andromache (an-drom'-a-kee). Wife of Hector and mother of Astyanax. After Hector died, she married his brother Helenus. Bore Molossus to Neoptolemus.

Aphrodite (af-ro-dye'-tee). Latin Venus. Goddess of love.

Apollo (a-pol'-ow). God of music, healing, and prophecy. Son of Zeus and Leto, twin brother of Artemis.

Arachneus (a-rak-nee'-us). Hill in Argolis near Mycenae.

Archelaus (ar-kel-ah'-us). King of Macedonia, patron of Euripides.

Ares (air'-ez). Latin Mars. God of war.

Argo (ar'-go). Jason's ship. His companions on his quest for the Golden Fleece were called the Argonauts.

Argos (ar'-gos). Strictly speaking, an ancient city, the capital of Argolis in the Peloponnese. But all the inhabitants of the Peloponnese, and even all the Greeks, are called Argives.

Aristaeus (a-ris-tay'-us). Son of Apollo and the nymph Cyrene. He married Autonoë; their son was Actaeon the famous hunter.

Artemis (ar'-te-mis). Latin Diana. Virgin goddess of hunting, prophecy, and childbirth. Daughter of Zeus and Leto, elder twin sister of Apollo.

Asopus (a-so'-pus). River in Thessaly.

Astyanax (as-tee'-a-nax). Young son of Hector and Andromache, killed at the fall of Troy. His name means "defender of the citadel."

Até (ah'-tay). The personification of moral blindness, daughter of Strife and sister of Lawlessness. She presides over (and can be a designation for) the act of someone, often in a state of Hubris; what follows is Nemesis.

Athena (a-thee'-na). Latin Minerva. Goddess of wisdom and patroness of Athens.

Athos (a'-thos). Mountain on the easternmost coast of Chalcis

Atreus (ay'-tree-us). Son of Pelops, father of Agamemnon and Menelaus, brother of Thyestes, whom he caused to eat the flesh of his own sons. (Or in some versions, he was the father of Pleisthenes and grandfather of Agamemnon and Menelaus.)

Aulis (owl'-is). Port in Boeotia where the Greek fleet gathered. The site of the sacrifice of Iphigenia.

Autonoë (au-ton'-oh-ee). Daughter of Cadmus who married Aristaeus, by whom she had Actaeon.

Axius (ax'-ee-us). River in Macedonia.

Bacchantes (bak-kan' teez). Also called Bacchae, the priestesses of Bacchus.

Bacchus (bak'-us). God of wine and drinking, son of Zeus and Semele. The Bacchanalia were his festivals.

Bactria (bak'-tree-a). Country of Asia, now part of Iran.

Boeotia (bee-oh'-sha). District in eastern Greece.

Bromius (bro'-mi-us). Name for Dionysus, meaning "the tumultuous one."

Cadmus (kad'-mus). Son of Agenor and sister of Europa. He established the country called Boeotia and founded the city of Thebes, which he populated with men (Spartoi) who sprung from the teeth of a dragon he had killed. He married Harmonia, and introduced the alphabet into Greece.

Calchas (kal'-kus). Soothsayer who accompanied the Greeks, and who told Agamemnon at Aulis that he must sacrifice his daughter Iphigenia.

Cassandra (ka-san'-dra). Daughter of Priam and Hecuba who was loved by Apollo. He gave her the gift of clairvoyance, but ruined the gift by wetting her lips with his tongue so that no one would ever believe her predictions.

Castor (kas'-tor). Son of Leda, brother of Pollux. The two are called the Dioscuri.

Centaurs (sen'-taurs). Creatures who were half human and half horse; lived in Thessaly.

Cephisus (ke'-fis-us). River on the Plain of Athens.

Charon (shar'-on). Ferryman of dead souls across the river Styx to Hades.

Chryseïs (cri-say'-us). Daughter of Chryses. She was taken by Agamemnon as his prize and then, after Apollo visited a plague on the Greeks, was returned to her father.

Chryses (kry'-sees). Priest of Apollo and father of Chryseïs.

Cithaeron (ki-thy'-ron). Mountain in Boeotia sacred to Zeus and the Muses.

Clytemnestra (kly-tem-nes'-tra). Daughter of Leda, sister of Helen, wife of Agamemnon, mistress of Aegisthus, and mother of Iphigenia, Orestes, and Electra.

Cocytus (ko-kee'-tus). River in Hades.

Colchis (kol'-kis). Country of Asia on the Black Sea, the birthplace of Medea.

Corinth (kor'-inth). City of Greece on the Isthmus of Corinth.

Corybantes (kor-i-ban'-teez). Priests of Cybele who were required to mu-
tilate themselves in order to be admitted to the service of the
goddess.

Corycus (kor'-i-kus). Mountain in Asia Minor, now called Curco.

Creon (kray'-on). Brother of Jocasta and king of Thebes after the death of
Polynices and Eteocles.

Cronus (kro'-nus). Latin Saturn.Titan, son of Heaven (Uranus) and Earth
(Gaia). He married his sister Rhea; their children included Demeter, Hades, Hera, Hestia, Poseidon, and Zeus, who overthrew
him.

Curetes (kur-ay'-teez). A people of Crete, also called Corybantes, who
dances enthusiastically. According to Ovid, they were produced
from rain.

Cybele (sib'-e-le). Daughter of Heaven and Earth, wife of Cronus. Her
priests were the Corybantes.

Cynossema (sin-o-sem'-a). Literally "dog's tomb," it is the Thracian head-
land where Hecuba was changed to a dog and buried.

Danaus (dan'-a-us). Son of Belus and Anchinoë and co-ruler of Egypt with
his brother Aegyptus. He came to the Peloponnese, where either
he usurped Gelanor's throne in Argos or, some say, Gelanor resigned the crown to him voluntarily.

Deiphobus (de-i-foh'-bus). Son of Priam and Hecuba. According to later
authors, he married Helen after the death of Paris.

Delos (del'-os). One of the Cyclades north of Naxos, island where Leto gave
birth to Apollo and Artemis.

Delphi (del'-fye). Town on the southwest side of Mount Parnassus where
the Pythia gave oracular messages inspired by Apollo.

Demeter (De-meet'-er). Latin Ceres. Earth-mother goddess of grains and
harvests. Her daughter was Persephone.

Dionysus (dee-oh-nee'-sus). Another name for Bacchus. The Dionysia was
the wine festival in the god's honor.

Dioscuri (dee-o-skur'-eye). The twins Castor and Pollux. Served as divine
messengers.

Dirce (dir'-see). Second wife of Lycus, king of Thebes. He married her after
divorcing Antiope. After the divorce, Antiope became pregnant by
Zeus, and Dirce, suspecting Lycus was the father, imprisoned and

tormented Antiope, who nonetheless escaped and bore Amphion and Zethus on Mount Cithaeron.

Dodona (do-doh´-na). Town in Epirus (some say Thessaly) where there was a temple to Zeus and the most ancient oracle of Greece. There was a grove of sacred oak trees surrounding the temple.

Echion (ek´-i-on). One of the men who sprang from the dragon's teeth Cadmus sowed. Father of Pentheus by Agave.

Electra (e-lek´-tra). Daughter of Agamemnon and Clytemnestra, sister of Orestes.

Eleutherai (el-oo´-the-rye). Boeotian village near Thebes.

Engia (en-gee´-a). Gulf of the Aegean Sea near Sunium.

Erechtheus (e-rek´-thee-us). Son of Pandion and the sixth king of Athens.

Erinyes (er-in´-yeez). The Furies, the spirits of divine vengeance, who later became the Eumenides.

Erythrae (e-rith´-ree). Town in Ionia opposite Chios.

Eros (air´-os). Latin Cupid. God of love.

Euboea (you-bee´-a). The long island that stretches from the Gulf of Pagasae to Andros, the chief cities of which were Chalcis and Eretria.

Eumenides (you-men´-i-deez). The name for the Erinyes in their benevolent aspect.

Eurotas (eu-roh´-tus). River near Sparta that the Spartans worshiped as a powerful god.

Furies. See Erinyes and Eumenides.

Gaia (guy´-a). Ancient personification of the earth. .

Geryon (ger´-yon). Monster with three bodies and three heads, killed by Heracles.

Glauce (glow´-kay). Wife of Jason after he divorced Medea.

Hades (hay´-deez). Latin Pluto. The world of the dead, or, sometimes, the god who ruled it.

Harmonia (har-mon´-ee-a). Daughter of Ares and Aphrodite, married Cadmus. Sometimes called Hermione.

Hecate (he´-ka-te or hek´-at). Goddess who presided over magic and witchcraft. Often conflated with Persephone and Artemis.

Hector (hek´-tor). Son of Priam and Hecuba, and the chief warrior of Troy. He married Andromache.

Hecuba (hek´-you-ba). Wife of Priam, mother of Hector, Paris, Helenus, Polydorus, Cassandra, Polyxena, and a number of other children.

Helen (hel'-en). Daughter of Leda, sister of Clytemnestra, wife of Menelaus, taken by Paris to Troy.

Helenus (hel'-en-us). Son of Priam and Hecuba, a soothsayer. He married Andromache, widow of his brother Hector.

Helios (heel'-i-os). Sun god, often conflated with Apollo.

Hellas (hel'-as). Name originally applied to a territory and a small tribe in southern Thessaly, it later came to include all Greeks.

Hephaestus (hef-fes'-tus). Latin Vulcan. God of fire and smithing.

Hera (her'-a). Latin Juno. Wife and sister of Zeus, and queen of heaven.

Heracles (her'-a-kleez). Latin Hercules. Son of Zeus by Alcmene. He was tormented by Hera and made to perform many arduous labors.

Hermes (her'-meez). Latin Mercury. Son of Zeus and Maia. He was the messenger god and patron of messengers and merchants.

Hermione (her-mye'-o-nee). Daughter of Menelaus and Helen. She was married to Neoptolemus but had no children by him. Eventually she married Orestes and had a son Tisamenus.

Hippolytus (hip-pol'-i-tus). Son of Theseus with whom his stepmother Phaedra falls in love.

Hubris (hoo'-bris). Overweening pride.

Hysiae (his'-ee-eye). Town in Boeotia.

Ida (eye'-da). Mountain near Troy; more properly, the whole ridge of mountains that are the source of the Simois, Scamander, Aesopus, and other rivers.

Ilium (il'-i-um) or Ilion. Name for Troy.

Ino (eye'-no). Daughter of Cadmus and Harmonia who nursed Bacchus.

Iolchus (yol'-kos). Town in Magnesia where Jason was born.

Iphigenia (if-i-jin-eye'-a). Daughter of Agamemnon and Clytemnestra whom he sacrificed at Aulis.

Ismenus (iz-may'-nus). River near Thebes.

Itys (it'-is). Son of Tereus, king of Thrace, and Procne. He was killed by his mother and served up as meat for his father. He was changed into a pheasant, his mother into a swallow, and his father into an owl.

Jason (jay'-son). Captain of the Argo whose life Medea saved and whom he married and then divorced.

Laconia. District of southern Greece of which Sparta was the capital.

Laertes (lay-air'-tees). Father of Odysseus.

Lapiths (la'-piths). Tribe of Thessaly who fought the Centaurs.

Lemnos (lem'-nos). Island in the Aegean Sea sacred to Hephaestus, now called Stalimine.

Leto (lee'-to). Titaness, daughter of Coeus and Phoebe, loved by Zeus to whom she bore Apollo and Artemis.

Loxias (lok'-see-us). Name for Apollo.

Lydia (lid'-i-a). Kingdom of Asia Minor.

Maenads (mee'-nads). The Bacchantes.

Maia (mye'-a). One of the Pleiades, mother of Hermes by Zeus.

Medea (mee-dee'-a). Daughter of Aeetes, king of Colchis, wife of Jason.

Media (mee'-dee-a). Country in Asia north of Persia.

Menelaus (me-ne-lay'-us). King of Sparta, son of Atreus, brother of Agamemnon, husband of Helen.

Moirae (moy'-rye). The three Fates, Clotho, Lachesis, and Atropos

Molossia (mo-los'-i-a). Country which Molossus ruled, famous for its dogs.

Molossus (mo-los'-us). Son of Neoptolemus and Andromache.

Muses. Goddesses of the arts, daughters of Zeus and Mnemosyne.

Mycenae (my-see'-nee). Town in the Peloponnese where Agamemnon ruled.

Neoptolemus (nee-op-tol'-e-mus). Also known as Pyrrhus. Son of Achilles, king of Epiru. He claimed Andromache as his prize after the fall of Troy.

Nereus (nee'-re-us). God of the sea who married Doris and with her had fifty daughters called the Nereids, who included Thetis and Psamanthe.

Niké (nee'-kay). Goddess of victory and therefore of sneakers.

Odysseus (o-dis'-yus). Latin Ulysses. King of Ithaca and one of the Greek heroes of the Trojan war.

Olympus (o-lim'-pus). Mountain of Thessaly so tall that the Greeks believed it touched the heavens; it was therefore the home of the Olympian gods.

Orestes (or-es'-teez). Son of Agamemnon and Clytemnestra, brother of Electra.

Orion (or-eye'-on). In the star myth, a giant hunter who pursued the

Pleiades and was in love with Eos (the Dawn). He was slain by Artemis and transformed into the constellation.

Orpheus (or'-fee-us). Son of Calliope and, some say, Apollo, who was so gifted with the lyre that even rivers stopped to listen to him.

Pallas (pal'-us). Name for Athena.

Pan. God of shepherds and hunters. He had horns and goat feet and invented the syrinx or reed flute.

Pandion (pan-dee'-on). Son of Erichton and king of Athens. He was the father of Philomela, Procne, Erectheus, and Butes.

Pandora (pan-dor'-a). According to Hesiod, the first mortal female, fashioned out of clay by Hephaestus. She received a box from Zeus she was to give to her husband. When she married Epimetheus and he opened the box, all the evils of the world flew out of it—perhaps including Elpis (hope).

Paphos (pa'-fos). City in Cyprus where Aphrodite rose from the sea; now Bafo.

Paris. Son of Priam and Hecuba who abducted Helen from Sparta and caused the Trojan war.

Parnassus (par-nas'-us). Mountain in Phocis, sacred to the Muses.

Peleus (pee'-lee-us). King of Thessaly who married Thetis. Achilles was their son.

Pelias (pee'-li-as). Son of Poseidon and Tyro and king of Iolcus. He murdered Aeson, his half-brother.

Pelion (pee'-lee-on). Mountain in Thessaly.

Peloponnese (pel-o-po-nees'). The large peninsula of southern mainland Greece.

Pelops (pee'-lops). Son of Tantalus, who cut him up and served him to the Phrygian gods.

Pentheus (pen'-thee-us). Son of Echion and Agave, king of Thebes who refused to acknowledge the divinity of Bacchus.

Pharsalia (far-sayl'-ya). Plain in Thessaly.

Pharsalus (far-sayl'-us). City in the Pharsalian plain.

Phasis (fas'-is). River of Colchis that flows into the Black Sea.

Phocis (foh'-kis). District of Greece next to Boeotia on the Gulf of Corinth.

Phocus (foh'-kus). Son of Aeacus and Psamanthe, killed by Telamon.

Phoebus (fee'-bus). Name for Apollo.

Phrygia (fri'-jee-a). Country in Asia Minor in which Troy was the most prominent city.

Phthia (fthee'-a). Birthplace of Achilles in Thessaly near Mt. Othrys.

Pieria (pye-eer'-ya). Part of Thessaly in which there was a spring the Muses frequented. They are therefore sometimes called Pierean.

Pittheus (pith'-e-us). King of Troezen in Argolis. Father of Aethra and grandfather of Theseus.

Pollux (pol'-ux). Twin brother of Castor, also called Polydeuces. See Dioscuri.

Polydeuces (pol-ee-doo'-seez). Alternate name for Pollux.

Polydorus (po-li-dor'-us). Youngest son of Priam and Hecuba, killed by his brother-in-law Polymestor.

Polymestor (po-li-mes'-tor). King of the Thracian peninsula who married Ilione, Priam's eldest daughter, and to whose care Priam and Hecuba entrusted Polydorus and a great treasure.

Polyxena (po-lix-ee'-na). Daughter of Priam and Hecuba. After the war she was sacrificed to Achilles' shade in a symbolic marriage.

Poseidon (po-sye'-don). Latin Neptune. God of the sea, brother of Demeter, Hades, Hera, Hestia, and Zeus.

Priam (pry'-am). King of Troy.

Procne (prok'-nee). Wife of Tereus, mother of Itys.

Proteus (pro'-tee-us). Sea god and king of Egypt, father of Theoclymenus.

Pylades (pye'-la-dees). Son of Strophius, companion and cousin of Orestes.

Pyrrhus (pir'-us). See Neoptolemus.

Pytho (pye'-tho). Ancient name of Delphi, called that because of the great serpent Apollo killed there.

Rhea (ree'-a). Titaness, wife of Cronus and mother of Zeus and his brothers and sisters.

Sardis (sar'-dis). Town at the foot of Mount Tmolus, capital of Lydia.

Saronic Gulf. The indentation of the sea opposite the Gulf of Corinth, with the Isthmus of Corinth between them.

Scylla (sil'-a). Daughter of Nisus whom she betrayed for the love of Minos, king of Crete. When the latter spurned her, she threw herself into the sea and was transformed to rocks dangerous to sailors.

Semele (sem'-e-le). Daughter of Cadmus and Harmonia, and, by Zeus, the mother of Bacchus.

Sepias (sep'i-as). Cape in Thessaly.

Simois (sim'-o-is). River near Troy.

Sisyphus (sis'-i-fus). Sufferer in Hades condemned to roll a huge stone up a mountain, a task repeated endlessly.

Skyros (skee'-ros). Island off Euboea.

Sophia (so-fee'-a). Goddess of wisdom

Strophius (stro'-fee-us). King of Phocis, brother-in-law of Agamemnon, and father of Pylades.

Symplegades (sim-pleg'-a-deez). Two small islands at the entrance of the Black Sea near the Bosphorus.

Talthybius (tal-thi'-bi-us). Herald of the Greeks.

Tauris (tor'-is). The Tauric peninsula to which Iphigenia was miraculously transported from Aulis.

Thebes (Theebz). City in Boeotia.

Themis (them'-is). Daughter of Uranus and Gaia who married Zeus and was the mother of Dike (justice), Irene (peace), Eunomia (good order), the Horae (the hours), and the Moirae (the fates).

Therapnae (ther-ap'-nee). City in Laconia near Sparta.

Theseus (thee'-see-us). Son of Aegeus and Aethra and king of Athens.

Thessaly (thes'a-lee). Territory to the north of Greece proper.

Thetis (thee'-tis). Nereid, wife of Peleus, mother of Achilles.

Thrace (Thrays). Area encompassing most of the world north of the Black Sea.

Thyestes (thy-es'-teez). Brother of Atreus, father of Aegisthus.

Tiresias (ti-rees'-i-us). Great prophet of Thebes who was turned into a woman and then back to a man. He was blinded by Athena because he caught sight of her bathing.

Tmolus (tmo'-lus). King of Lydia, or the mountain on which he is buried.

Troezen (tree'-zen). Town in Argolis in the Peloponnese.

Uranus (you'-ra-nus). Ancient personification of the sky, produced by and then consort of Gaia, overcome by his son Cronus.

Xenios (ksen'-yos). Epithet for Zeus calling attention to his special interest in the sacred host-guest relationship.

Zeus (zoos). Latin Jupiter. Son of the Titans Cronus and Rhea, brother of Demeter, Hades, Hera (whom he married), Hestia, and Poseidon. After he overthrew Cronus he became the chief Greek god.

About the Translators

I N É S   A Z A R holds a Ph.D. degree in Romance languages from Johns Hopkins University and is a graduate of the University of Buenos Aires, where she studied classics and linguistics and subsequently taught those subjects. She has published two books, one on the classical tradition in Renaissance poetry, and a group of poems written in conversation with the figure of Medea. Since 1971 she has taught at George Washington University.

D A N I E L   M A R K   E P S T E I N is a poet, essayist, and dramatist with ten books in print; his poetry includes *The Boy in the Well* (1995), *Spirits* (1987), *The Book of Fortune* (1982), and *Young Men's Gold* (1979). His writing has also appeared in the *Atlantic,* the *New Yorker,* the *New Republic* and other magazines and anthologies. His dramas *Jenny and the Phoenix* and *The Midnight Visitor* have been performed in regional theater and off-Broadway. His translation from the Latin of Plautus' comic play *Trinnumus* was published in the Complete Roman Drama in Translation series. His awards include a Guggenheim Fellowship and the Prix de Rome from the American Academy of Arts and Letters.

D O N A L D   J U N K I N S graduated from the University of Massachusetts in 1953. After teaching at Boston University, Emerson College, and Chico State College, he returned to Amherst, where he has taught for thirty years. He has published nine books of poems—including *Playing for Keeps, The Agamenticus Poems, Crossing by Ferry: Poems New and Selected,* and *The Uncle Harry Poems and Other Maine Reminiscences*—and an anthology of contemporary world poets. He is a frequent guest reader and lecturer in school and university settings throughout the world, from the Bahamas to China.

MARILYN NELSON holds postgraduate degrees from the University of Pennsylvania and the University of Minnesota, and is a professor of English at the University of Connecticut, Storrs. She has published five books—*For the Body, Mama's Promises, The Homeplace, Magnificat,* and *The Fields of Praise*—in addition to two collections of verse for children. Her honors include a Kent fellowship, two Pushcart prizes, two creative writing fellowships from the National Endowment for the Arts, an individual artist's grant from the Connecticut Commission for the Arts, the 1990 Connecticut Arts Award, and a 1995 Fulbright Teaching Fellowship in France. Her third book, *The Homeplace,* was a finalist for the 1991 National Book Award and won the 1992 Annisfield-Wolf Award.

ELEANOR WILNER has published four volumes of peotry, most recently *Otherwise* (1993). Her work has appeared in more than a dozen anthologies and some thirty periodicals in the United States, England, and Japan. A graduate of Goucher College with M.A. and Ph.D. degrees from Johns Hopkins University, she has served as editor of *American Poetry Review* and as a radio and newspaper feature writer. She has taught at the University of Hawaii, the University of Chicago, the University of Iowa, Temple University Japan, Goucher College, and elsewhere. Her honors include a MacArther Foundation Fellowship and fellowships from the Pennsylvania Council on the Arts and the National Endowment for the Arts. She has won the Warren Fine Poetry Prize, the Juniper Prize, and a Borestone Mountain Poetry Award.